HEALING
CODEPENDENCY

*How to Resolve Your Childhood Trauma
so You Can Start Living Your Best Life*

Elena Miro

Copyright info

© Copyright Elena Miro 2023 - All rights reserved.

The content contained within this book may not be reproduced, duplicated, or transmitted without direct written permission from the author or the publisher except for the use of brief quotations in a book review.

Under no circumstances will any blame or legal responsibility be held against the publisher, or author, for any damages, reparation, or monetary loss due to the information contained within this book. Either directly or indirectly. You are responsible for your own choices, actions, and results.

<u>Legal Notice:</u>

This book is copyright protected. This book is only for personal use. You cannot amend, distribute, sell, use, quote or paraphrase any part, or the content within this book, without the consent of the author or publisher except for the use of brief quotations in a book review.

<u>Disclaimer notice:</u>

Please note the information contained within this book is for educational and entertainment purposes only. All effort has been executed to present accurate, up to date, and reliable, complete information. No warranties of any kind are declared or implied. Readers acknowledge that the author is not engaging in the rendering of legal, financial, medical, or professional advice. The content within this book has been derived from various sources. Please consult a licensed professional before attempting any techniques outlined in this book.

By reading this book, the reader agrees that under no circumstances is the author responsible for any losses, direct or indirect, which are incurred as a result of the use of the information contained within this book, including, but not limited to,—errors, omissions, or inaccuracies.

Table of Contents

Chapter 1: Who Built You? 9

Chapter 2: Exploring Within to Heal Throughout 23

Chapter 3: Identifying Emotional Triggers and Wounds ... 41

Chapter 4: What Your Inner Child Needs 62

Chapter 5: Embrace Your Shadow Self 79

Chapter 6: Becoming Your Own Hero 97

Chapter 7: Resolving Old, Toxic Relationships 120

Chapter 8: The Road to a Happier You 141

Chapter 9: New Habits, New Life 160

Chapter 10: Keeping It Real 178

References Cited 185

A Word Before We Begin

———•◇•———

The road to healing your codependency can sometimes be rough. When I began this journey, I was in a state of confusion and pain. Overwhelmed by a deep sense of confusion, I battled with depression, sensing that something within me was amiss, yet struggling to pinpoint its exact nature. My emotional anguish ran deep, amplified by the recent dissolution of a toxic narcissistic marriage, leaving me feeling adrift and devoid of purpose. My emotional anguish ran deep, amplified by my divorce from a toxic narcissist, leaving me feeling adrift and devoid of purpose. I couldn't see a clear path to healing, and I didn't even really know what it was that I was looking for at that time. I was wounded, depressed, and numb. The innate sense of independence that had always defined me seemed elusive, leaving me disconnected both from others and my own spirit. I was going through a rapid change in my life, but the way forward was shrouded in darkness. I couldn't see what I needed to do with clear eyes.

As I began to examine my behavioral patterns, talk with experts in psychology, and educate myself on behavioral problems, I started discerning a trend of people pleasing that I most definitely did not want to admit. I had always thought of myself as strong-willed and independent person. In fact, many people in my life had told me the same thing. But there it was—I was seeing more clearly just how codependent I actually was and just how much I needed the approval of others. A realization dawned on me: what I was seeking from other people was really what I needed to give to myself. As the patterns of codependency unfolded before my eyes, I knew that I needed to go more profound, as painful as it could be. But I knew something else; I knew the healing would be worth the pain. I knew that facing that emotional pain was but a brief stepping stone that would ultimately lead to a much happier, healthier me. And it has. I earned my degree in psychology and began counseling other people in need. I became strongly motivated to help everyone escape the bonds of their psychological problems, so they could become happier too. Healing myself was a huge part of what motivated me to help others heal as well. You can have a happier life that's more in-line with your dreams and goals, and even more than that, you *deserve* to have that life.

This book is organized to help you through healing your codependency, so you can get started on your own dreams. I know that I appreciated books like this when I began my journey because they helped me to realize that my emotions were perfectly normal. Additionally, they helped me to realize that I was not alone. So many people are experiencing the same thing as we are that there isn't a big enough concert hall in the world to hold us all. Codependency is a common behavioral pattern, and it makes sense from the perspective of a social species. We live in groups, and that helps us survive. But living in groups means compromising and pleasing others to some degree. It's when we are so focused on pleasing other people that we forget to take care of ourselves that we have a problem. And many of us have that same problem, but it can be healed.

In this book, I will guide you through a transformative journey. You will gain insight into the intricacies of your being, unravel the mysteries behind your unique self, inner child, and shadow self, explore the inner pain that resides within you—and learn how to become your own hero. With the aid of these techniques that I will impart to you, you can liberate yourself from the confines of the prison constructed by your conditioned behavior. Once you can do that, then you can truly resolve those old, toxic relationships. You can then set goals toward the life you've always wanted to have. You'll have new habits and new coping strategies for dealing with stress and disappointment, which will help you interact with other people while still focusing on your own priorities. You don't have to give up your dreams to help someone else. In fact, if you *do* give up what you want, you won't be able to help others. I'll show you why that's true and how to avoid this self-sacrificing trap.

Once you acquire these skills, I'll help you learn how to maintain them for the rest of your life, so you don't fall back into your old ways. It might seem like an impossible task at the outset, but I can assure you that if you stick with it, you'll start seeing positive results immediately. As you take care of your needs, you will feel a growing sense of self-worth and self-appreciation. You'll also notice that when you respect yourself, other people will respect you as well. That's not to say there won't be bad days—but you'll develop new, healthier coping strategies for those challenging moments. Your life will improve exponentially, and I know because I've been through it. I couldn't believe I would ever feel significantly different, and no one was more surprised than I was when I started seeing changes in others' behavior since I'd been putting my own needs first. It changes your life in ways that you may be unable to imagine right now, but soon, what you can't imagine will be a reality.

The most important thing to remember is that you are not alone. Many people are in the same situation as you, and they are all also starting their own healing journeys. Together, we can change our reality. Together, we can make life what we *really* want it to be. Together, we can make a difference in the world—through changing how we treat ourselves. It quite simply makes the world a better place, one brave soul at a time. So take my hand, and let's start the journey toward a happier, healthier life and a better world for everyone…

Chapter 1

Who Built You?

We often talk about building our houses or even our lives, but there are ways in which our lives—our childhood home and experiences—also build us. Construction begins with your very first breath and experiencing the world around you. Of course, it can also be argued that you first learn about the world while you're still nestled in your mother's womb. Her fears infuse your newly forming body with an estimate of what the world will be like when you arrive. Research has found, in fact, that the uterine environment is a dynamic place wherein the mother and fetus are in a constant state of communication and adjustment. Even at such a tender state of development, construction has begun on the unique entity that will become you. However, after you're born, that process accelerates. In my first book on codependency, *Am I a People Pleaser? Codependency and the Childhood Trauma that Creates Relationship*

Addicts, I discussed attachment theory and how you form your foundational perspective of the world around you in the first two to three years of your life. Let me give you a brief overview.

You can think of attachment theory as analogous to the childhood story of the *Three Little Pigs*. Attachment theory relates to how you come to view the world. It's your foundation for how you will proceed when making certain choices. People whose mothers or other primary caregivers respond to their needs quickly and satisfyingly develop secure attachment styles. Their choices are born from a foundation wherein they believe that the world is a safe place where their needs will usually be met, and they respond to crises in accordance with that belief. They have been built into a solid house of brick by the people and experiences around them. When the wolf comes to their door, he can huff and puff all he likes, but he won't be able to blow their house down. That sounds like magical thinking to someone like me, who developed an insecure attachment style. People whose primary caregivers were slow to meet their needs or perhaps neglected them altogether may view the world as unsafe and unable to meet their needs. This is where I live, and I don't live there alone; most with codependency have an insecure attachment style. The basis for our choices comes from a place of fear and insecurity. The experiences and people who built us weren't careful in their construction techniques; they cut corners and used straw and wood for materials. The most fearful among us are constructed of straw, and the wolf is easily able to blow us over. Some of us are made of wood, but the wolf can still blow us over with a little more energy. This is the basis for many psychological problems, including patterns of codependent behaviors. But let's go deeper yet—into the human psyche.

__The Birth of Desire: Sigmund Freud and the Human Psyche__

According to psychologist Sigmund Freud, the human psyche is made up of three parts: the Id, the Ego, and the Super-ego.

The Id is basically the primitive, instinctual part of our mind. It includes our libido—or sexual drives—as well as our aggressive drives. It also includes our hidden memories. The Super-ego is our moral compass. It is the part of our mind that incorporates the values and morals we learn from our parents and our culture. It is the part of us that doles out rewards in the form of, for example, feelings of pride or satisfaction; likewise, it also meets out punishment, manifested as emotions like shame and guilt. Finally, the Ego is the part of our mind that mediates between the primitive desires of the Id and the moral guidelines of the Super-ego. The Id is impulsive and infantile and changes little over time. It does not operate on logic—it is best described as fantasy-oriented. The Ego is the only part of this trio that we are consciously aware of; it is what we think of when we think of ourselves. It is the decision-making component of our mind that operates on the reality principle as it tries to satisfy both the baser urges of the Id and the strict moral codes of the Super-ego.

The Super-ego includes two systems: the conscience and the ideal self. These aspects of the self are what a person would use to push toward perfection. The conscience tells us when we've done something wrong; the ideal self encompasses the mental construct of who you aspire to be, which includes an intricate portrayal that encompasses your professional ambitions, perspectives on how you treat others, and the expectations of societal behavior.

We incorporate the norms taught by our parents and the society in which we live into our Super-ego, which then acts as our moral compass. It's not something we're necessarily consciously aware of, although if asked, we can certainly recite our moral norms. That doesn't mean, however, that we can fully understand how they are guiding our behavior. Regardless of societal norms, each of us harbors a primordial essence—a fundamental element woven into the very fabric of our consciousness—comprising our instincts and untamed desires, which have been indelibly imprinted over countless ages of evolutionary influence.

This is the Id—it encompasses the behaviors and drives that have contributed to individual generational success, thus resulting in a thriving population well-adapted to their environment. As humans, our environment includes the whole world; thus, our range of successful behaviors, and their subsequent instinctual drives, can be quite broad. We are rarely aware of drives beyond insatiable urges or desires. You might, for example, have an insatiable desire for sugar. You know you want it every time you see it, and even at times when you don't. You might attribute it to the addictive nature of processed sugar, but it actually goes back to a basic, evolutionarily guided drive. In our distant ancestors who were forced to live off the land and suffered from seasonal starvation, sugar was a rare albeit valuable resource due to its high caloric content. As a result, [humans evolved a "thrifty gene"](#) that codes sugar cravings, so when it is available, they would eat all that they could get, which would then give them stored fat to carry them through lean times. Now, in an age of overabundance, it is causing problems like obesity and diabetes. Knowing that doesn't kill the craving, however. It's a desire that's been coded in your genes and manifested in your Id beyond the ages.

Between these two mechanisms—the Super-ego and the Id—there is the Ego. This is your conscious awareness of self. Though conscious, it's still guided by unconscious forces working through the Super-ego and the Id; the Ego strives to mediate the two. You can view it as the mediator bargaining between two parties in a lawsuit. The Super-ego demands adherence to a certain moral code, whereas the Id wants what it wants, and it wants it *now!* The Ego tries to appease both sides. You can already probably see numerous ways in which this system might go awry, particularly in a dysfunctional family environment where extremes are the norm. As a codependent, you are torn by your Id's primitive, instinctual need for human connection—the result of generations of evolutionary forces at work on a social organism—and the values instilled in your Super-ego by the people and experiences who built you. So who were they, and what kind of materials did they use?

The Blueprint to Build You

The blueprint for building you began with your first interactions with your primary caregivers. Whether or not they mirrored loving, caring emotions or neglectful, negative emotions, that all formed the basis for your first impressions of the world. Mirroring is imitating or reflecting the emotions, expressions, and behaviors of another person. It is a natural and essential part of human communication and social interaction. Mirroring plays a crucial role in the development of infants, as it helps them form secure attachments, learn social skills, and build self-awareness. Attachment is, as we have discussed, the emotional bond that forms between an infant and their primary caregiver, usually a mother. Attachment provides the infant with a sense of security, comfort, and trust. Mirroring is one way that caregivers can foster attachment with their infants. By mirroring the infant's facial expressions, vocalizations, and movements, the caregiver shows that they are attentive, responsive, and empathetic to the infant's needs and feelings. This creates a positive feedback loop that reinforces the attachment bond. Mirroring also helps the infant regulate their emotions and cope with stress. For example, when an infant cries, the caregiver can mirror their distress, and then soothe them with a calm voice and a gentle touch. This shows the infant that they are not alone and that their emotions are valid and manageable.

Learning in infants is acquiring new knowledge, skills, and abilities through observation, imitation, and feedback. Learning is essential for the survival and adaptation of infants in their environment, particularly for pre-verbal infants. Mirroring facilitates learning by providing infants with models to imitate and feedback to improve. By mirroring the actions and words of their caregivers and others around them, infants learn how to perform various tasks and communicate effectively. For example, when an infant sees their caregiver smiling and saying "hello," they can mirror their expression and sound and learn how to greet someone. Mirroring also helps infants to learn about cause and effect, social norms, and moral values; when an infant sees their caregiver reacting positively or negatively to certain behaviors, they can mirror their emotion and learn what is acceptable or unacceptable. This is a vital step in eventually developing identity.

Identity is the perception of oneself that evolves gradually as a result of developing self-awareness, self-recognition, and self-esteem, and is important for the psychological well-being and social integration of infants. Mirroring supports identity development by offering infants feedback on themselves and their relationships. Through mirroring in a mirror or camera, caregivers aid infants in recognizing their distinct individuality, fostering self-awareness and self-recognition. Additionally, caregivers can nurture infants' positive self-image and self-esteem by mirroring their qualities and accomplishments in a supportive and encouraging manner. This then fosters self-confidence and self-respect. Moreover, mirroring is beneficial not only for infants, but also for caregivers, as it enhances their emotional connection, mutual understanding, and satisfaction with their relationship. Mirroring also contributes to introjection.

Introjection is a psychological process in which a person unconsciously incorporates the attitudes, values, or behaviors of another person or group into their own self-concept. Introjection can be seen as a form of identification, but it differs from identification in that it involves a passive and uncritical acceptance of external influences rather than an active and selective assimilation of them. Introjection can have both positive and negative effects on your personality and mental health, depending on the nature and source of the introjected material. One of the main functions of introjection is to protect the ego from anxiety or guilt by internalizing the standards and expectations of others. For example, a child who is scolded by their parents for doing something wrong may introject their parents' voices and repeat the same criticism to themselves whenever they make a mistake. Doing so can help the child avoid further punishment and conform to social norms, but it can also lead to low self-esteem and excessive self-criticism in adulthood. Similarly, a person who is rejected or abandoned by a romantic partner may introject their partner's negative evaluation of them and believe that they are unworthy of love or happiness.

Another function of introjection is coping with loss or separation by preserving a bond with the lost object or person. For example, a person who loses a loved one may introject their memories, traits, or values into their personality and continue to act as if they were still present. On the one hand, this can help that person maintain connection and continuity with the deceased; on the other hand, it can also prevent them from grieving properly and moving on with their life. In some cases, introjection can lead to pathological forms of identification, such as delusions or hallucinations. Introjection can also be viewed as a means of broadening your perception of the self by incorporating desirable or admired aspects of others. For example, a person who admires a celebrity may introject their style, mannerisms, or opinions into their own behavior and expression. They can then enhance their personal identity and confidence; however, it can also result in a loss of authenticity and individuality. Moreover, introjection can create unrealistic or idealized expectations that can be difficult to fulfill or sustain.

To achieve a healthy and balanced personality, you need to be aware of introjection and its effects on your perception on the self. You need to distinguish between your thoughts and feelings and those derived from others. You need to evaluate the sources and validity of the introjected material critically and reject or modify any harmful or inappropriate material. Additionally, you need to integrate positive and useful aspects of introjection into your identity while maintaining autonomy and differentiation from others. This can prove challenging when dealing with specific aspects of early-life introjected emotions. Introjected feelings can be subtle and difficult to discern. For example, my own mother's negativity and her inability to care for my needs were something I introjected at a very young age in the form of feeling inadequate or unworthy. I was never enough. But what about you?

Exercise #1

So, Who Made You?

This exercise is designed to help you recognize your attachment style and possible introjected emotions. Once you've identified them, the second part will address ways you can heal negative influences.

Part 1

Identifying

One way to determine your attachment style and introjected emotions is to use the following exercise:

1. Think of a significant person in your life, such as a parent, partner, friend, or sibling. Write down their name and your relationship with them.
2. Recall a recent, emotionally charged interaction with this person, either positive or negative. Write down what happened, how you felt, what you said, and what they said.
3. Consider how this interaction mirrors or exemplifies your attachment style with this person. Use the four categories of attachment styles: secure, anxious, avoidant, or fearful. Write down which category best describes your attachment style and why.
4. Identify any introjected emotions that you experienced during or after the interaction. Introjected emotions are emotions that you have internalized from others, such as guilt, shame, anger, or fear. Write down which introjected emotions you felt and where they came from.
5. Evaluate how your attachment style and introjected emotions affect your relationship with this person and yourself. Write down what you would like to change or improve in your attachment style and introjected emotions, as well as the steps you can take to achieve those changes.

This exercise can provide valuable insight into your attachment style, introjected emotions, and their impact on your interpersonal dynamics as well as self-esteem. For a more comprehensive understanding of your attachment patterns and emotional regulation, you can replicate this exercise with various other individuals in your life.

Part 2

Healing

This exercise is designed to help you heal negative introjected emotions and insecure attachment styles, with the objective to practice self-compassion and positive affirmations. Self-compassion is the ability to treat yourself with kindness, understanding, and acceptance, especially when facing difficulties or failures. Positive affirmations are statements that reinforce your strengths, values, and worthiness.

To practice self-compassion and positive affirmations, you can follow these steps:

1. Identify a situation that triggers negative emotions or insecurity in you. For example, you may feel ashamed of making a mistake at work or anxious about losing your partner's love.
2. Notice how you talk to yourself about the situation. Do you use harsh, critical, or blaming words? Do you exaggerate the negative aspects or ignore the positive ones? Do you compare yourself unfavorably to others or doubt your abilities? Write down examples of any negative self-talk you may have.

3. Imagine how you would talk to a friend in the same situation. What words of comfort, support, or encouragement would you use? How would you help them see the situation more realistically and constructively? Write down examples of positive statements you would make.
4. Replace your self-talk with the friend-talk. Use the same words and tone you would use with a friend. Acknowledge your feelings without judging them and remind yourself of your strengths and achievements. Express gratitude for what you have and hope for what you want. Do this actively; don't just think about it. Look at yourself in the mirror as you say the words out loud.
5. Repeat this exercise whenever you encounter a challenging situation or feel insecure in your relationships.

Over time, you will develop a more positive and compassionate relationship with yourself and others. You will retrain your brain to use positive self-talk anytime you're confronted with negative emotions and situations.

Final Thoughts on Who Made You

As you delve into your early life experiences that led to negative introjected emotions and insecure attachment styles, you may also confront difficult emotions that impact your daily life. This is normal and to be expected, so be gentle with yourself when this happens. Take a moment to excuse yourself from any interactions you're currently having and sit with your emotions for a moment. Tell yourself that your emotions are valid and that you want to deal with them properly. Make a commitment to yourself to delve into the depth of your experiences when the timing is right, and ensure that you follow through on this pledge. This is how you will heal, and it will be the most important thing you will ever do. It colors all of your other life experiences, so treat it with the appropriate level of respect, kindness, and self-love that you have always deserved. You didn't always get it, but now, you can give it to yourself. This is just the beginning of exploring your inner emotional landscape, so it's vital that you establish a strong foundation of self-respect and self-love. Doing so will carry you through what's to come.

Chapter 2

Exploring Within to Heal Throughout

Healing codependency is, as they say, an inside job. You have to go deep inside to discover the source of your wounds and how those scars shaped your behavior. The truth is not out there; it's *in* there. It's inside, and going to that inside place will be one of the most difficult journeys you'll ever make. It will, however, also be one of the most rewarding. To heal your codependent patterns of behavior, it is crucial to embark on an inward exploration. As you uncover the underlying origins of your thought patterns and behaviors, you can begin the process of healing those wounds and transforming your behaviors.

What Do You Truly Believe?

Back when my mother would criticize me relentlessly at a young age, I would adopt certain assumptions about myself. I started believing that I was worthless, stupid, inept, and unworthy of love. Core beliefs, which develop during childhood, significantly influence our interpersonal behaviors; for me, specifically, they contributed to my pursuit of self-love through the validation of others. They are fundamental assumptions that shape how we perceive ourselves, others, and the world. These beliefs form as a result of our experiences and interactions with family, peers, teachers, and other influential individuals. Core beliefs can be positive or negative, and they can have a profound impact on how a person thinks, feels, and behaves throughout their life.

Codependent patterns of behavior are often rooted in core beliefs formed in childhood and reinforced by dysfunctional relationships. Some common core beliefs that can produce codependent patterns of behavior include:

- I am not good enough.
- I have to please others to be loved.
- I am responsible for other people's happiness and problems.
- I have to sacrifice my needs for others.
- I have no control over my life.
- I need someone else to make me feel complete.

These core beliefs can lead to codependent behaviors, such as:

- Being overly dependent on or attached to someone else.

- Trying to fix, rescue, or save someone else from their issues.
- Neglecting or suppressing one's own needs, feelings, and desires.
- Having poor boundaries and allowing others to violate them.
- Feeling guilty, ashamed, or resentful when saying no or setting limits.
- Having low self-esteem and self-worth.
- Being afraid of rejection, abandonment, or conflict.
- Having difficulty expressing one's own opinions, preferences, or emotions.

These codependent behaviors can have negative consequences on your mental health, well-being, and relationships, and they can cause stress, anxiety, depression, anger, resentment, loneliness, isolation, and dissatisfaction. They can also prevent you from achieving goals, fulfilling your potential, and living authentically. The first step to breaking free from codependent patterns of behavior is to identify and challenge any core beliefs that underlie them. This can be done with the help of a therapist, support group, or self-help program. By changing your core beliefs, you can then change your perspective, attitude, and behaviors. You can learn to:

- Accept yourself as you are and value yourself as a person.

- Recognize and meet your own needs, feelings, and desires.
- Establish and maintain healthy boundaries with others.
- Communicate assertively and respectfully with others.
- Develop autonomy and agency over your own life.
- Seek healthy and fulfilling relationships with others.

Core beliefs are not always easy to uncover however, since they are often subconscious and automatic—which would mean that they are not easily accessible or questioned by the conscious mind. They act as filters that influence how a person perceives and interprets reality. For instance, a person with the core belief that they are incompetent and inadequate may attribute their successes to luck or external factors and their failures to their own flaws or shortcomings. They may also avoid taking risks or pursuing opportunities that could challenge their core beliefs and expose them to failure or criticism. Moreover, they may be completely unaware of these patterns. They're not consciously thinking, "I'm attributing my successes to luck and my inadequacies to my own flaws;" they're doing it automatically. It's a habit.

By acknowledging those negative core beliefs, you can establish healthier and more positive habits, ultimately leading to a complete transformation of your behavior.

For example, a person who believes that they are incompetent and inadequate may learn to recognize their strengths and achievements habitually, acknowledge their limitations and areas for improvement, and accept themselves as a person capable of learning and growing. They can then see that it's not an inherent flaw in their character; their behavior is just the result of learned conditioning that they accepted as true. When you've been told enough times that you're stupid, you start believing that must be true. Once you start challenging that assumption, you will then see that you're not stupid at all. You might be ignorant or make poor decisions, but that does not equate to stupidity.

Recognizing the Problem

Recognizing our core beliefs can help us understand why we react the way we do to certain situations, and we can also then challenge the limiting or negative ones. One way to recognize our core beliefs is to identify the thoughts that pop up in our mind when we face a problem or a stressful event. These thoughts are often distorted or exaggerated and reflect our underlying beliefs. For example, if we fail a test and think, "I'm stupid and worthless," we may have a core belief that we are not good enough or that we need to be perfect. What is your inner dialogue like? Another way to recognize our core beliefs is to examine our emotional and behavioral patterns over time. If we notice that we often feel anxious, depressed, angry, or insecure, we may have some core beliefs that are causing us distress. Similarly, if we notice that we tend to avoid certain situations, people, or activities, some of our core beliefs may be holding us back from living fully. The next time you decide you don't want to go to that family gathering or dinner with your friends, ask yourself if your decision is really based on your introverted nature (nothing wrong with that) or because you think they will find you boring. If it is the latter case, it is possible that you have internalized a limiting core belief that is impeding your progress.

A third way to recognize our core beliefs is to trace them back to their origins. Core beliefs are usually formed in childhood or adolescence as a result of experiences with our family, peers, teachers, and society. They may also be influenced by our culture, religion, gender, and personality. By reflecting their development, we can gain more insight into their validity and usefulness. Recognizing our core beliefs is the first step toward changing them. Once we identify them, we can evaluate them objectively and challenge them with evidence and alternative perspectives. We can also replace them with more positive and realistic ones that can support our well-being and growth. We can then improve our self-esteem, confidence, and happiness.

Changing Your Core Beliefs

Core beliefs can be positive or negative and can be helpful or unhelpful in different situations. However, some core beliefs are rigid, distorted, or unrealistic and can cause us to suffer unnecessarily or limit our potential.

Changing core beliefs is not easy, but it is possible with consistent effort and practice. Here are some steps you can follow to identify and modify your core beliefs:

1. **Identify your core beliefs:** You can do this by paying attention to your automatic thoughts and making note of any themes or patterns that emerge. For example, if you often think, "I'm not good enough" or "I always fail," you might have a core belief of being inadequate or incompetent.
2. **Challenge your core beliefs:** You can achieve this by seeking evidence that either challenges or reinforces your core beliefs. For example, if you have a core belief of being inadequate, you can list some of your achievements or strengths that prove otherwise. You can also ask yourself questions like "Is this belief true?" "Is this belief helpful?" "Where did this belief come from?" and "What would I tell a friend who had this belief?"
3. **Replace your core beliefs.** You can achieve this by developing new core beliefs that reflect your authentic values and goals while also being realistic and adaptable. For example, instead of believing "I'm not good enough," you can replace it with "I'm worthy of respect and love" or "I can learn from my mistakes and grow."

You can also use affirmations, visualization, or other techniques to reinforce your new core beliefs.
4. **<u>Practice your new core beliefs:</u>** You act in ways that are consistent with your new core beliefs and noticing how they affect your emotions and behaviors. For instance, if you embrace the core belief that you are capable, you can push yourself to explore new experiences and take on additional responsibilities. You can also reward yourself for your efforts and achievements and celebrate your progress.

Changing core beliefs takes time and patience, but it can impact your well-being and happiness profoundly. By identifying, challenging, replacing, and practicing new core beliefs, you can then transform your self-image and outlook on life.

Learning to Accept Who You Really Are

Understanding and changing negative core beliefs is a big part of exploring your inner psyche, but there's another important component of this work that is vital to healing. Most codependents, such as myself, don't think of themselves as worthy—worthy of love, respect, or kindness. As proof, they point to the flaws and mistakes they've made. Usually, these are things that someone in your life has pointed out many times in the past. Learning to accept who you are is one of the most crucial aspects of personal growth and happiness. It means recognizing your strengths and weaknesses, values and beliefs, emotions and motivations, and dreams and aspirations. It also means accepting your limitations and challenges, mistakes and failures, and flaws and imperfections. Accepting who you are does not mean settling for less or giving up on yourself; it means being honest and realistic about yourself and embracing your uniqueness and diversity. It means loving yourself, no matter your flaws or mistakes you make; you love yourself just because you are worthy of love.

There are many benefits of learning to accept who you are. First, it can enhance your self-esteem and confidence by freeing you from the habit of comparing yourself to others or seeking external validation. You can appreciate your worth and potential and celebrate your achievements and progress. Second, it can improve your mental health and well-being since you are reducing stress and anxiety. You are also coping better with challenges and setbacks and cultivating more positive emotions. Additionally, you can cultivate a mindset that is more balanced and adaptable, steering clear of negative thoughts and behaviors such as self-criticism, perfectionism, and procrastination. Third, it can enhance your relationships with others by communicating more authentically and respectfully, expressing your needs and boundaries more clearly, and empathizing more deeply with others. Furthermore, you have the ability to draw in individuals who are supportive and compatible, foster healthier relationships, and approach conflict resolution more constructively.

Learning to accept who you are is not always easy or straightforward, however. It requires courage and commitment, as well as patience and compassion. It is a lifelong process that involves constant reflection, feedback, experimentation, and adaptation. Here are some tips to help you learn to accept who you are:

- **<u>Identify your core values and beliefs:</u>** These principles will serve as the guiding force behind your decisions and actions, reflecting the utmost importance of what truly matters to you in life. They can be based on your personal experiences, cultural background, spiritual beliefs, or moral convictions. Knowing your core values and beliefs can help you align your actions with your purpose and thus live more authentically and meaningfully. It helps you to live with integrity.
- **<u>Recognize your strengths and weaknesses:</u>** These are the qualities that make you good or bad at certain tasks or situations. They can be related to your skills, talents, knowledge, personality traits, or habits. Understanding your strengths and weaknesses can aid in leveraging your assets, improving areas for growth, and selecting goals and activities aligned with your abilities and interests. This is all in good sentiment, but acknowledging weaknesses can be difficult because it can be hard to admit your

flaws. For example, I wish I could sing, but one of my weaknesses is that I don't have a good voice. That doesn't make me a bad person or that I can't express myself musically; it just means that I shouldn't quit my day job for a singing career—which is entirely okay! I can acknowledge that weakness and focus my efforts, including my musical expression, elsewhere.

- **Acknowledge your emotions and motivations:** These are the feelings that influence one's mood and behavior and the reasons that drive you to do or avoid something. They can be based on your needs, desires, fears, hopes, or expectations. Recognizing your emotions and motivations helps you better manage your impulses and reactions while also helping you understand what brings you happiness or unhappiness. For example, as a codependent, you might recognize that you have a tendency to feel unhappy unless you are helping serve someone else's needs. When you can acknowledge that motivation and the emotions behind it, you can then find ways to help others without neglecting your own needs. Assisting others isn't the bad part of codependency. It is when your self-worth becomes reliant on the compulsion to help others that a positive trait can turn into a vulnerability. Recognizing that can be the key to freeing yourself.

- **Explore your dreams and aspirations:** These are the visions that inspire you to pursue something bigger or better in life. They can be related to your career, education, family, health, hobbies, or social causes. Recognizing your dreams and aspirations can help you set meaningful goals and plan realistic strategies to achieve them. Most codependents put aside their dreams and aspirations in favor of fostering someone else's. But that doesn't serve you, and in the end, it doesn't serve them. To be of genuine service to others, you first have to realize your own dreams and work toward making them your reality.
- **Accept your limitations and challenges:** These are the factors that may hinder or prevent you from doing or reaching a goal. They can be related to your physical conditions, mental health issues, financial constraints, social barriers, or environmental obstacles. Accepting your limitations and challenges does not mean giving up on or ignoring them; it means being aware of them and finding ways to overcome or adapt to them. For example, you might have to accept that you don't have the money to get a specific degree, but that doesn't mean you can't learn what you need to know for your dream job. You can still approach getting that dream job from a different perspective.

- **Accept your mistakes and failures:** These are the outcomes that do not meet your expectations or standards. They can be related to your performance, judgment, behavior, or communication. Accepting your mistakes and failures does not mean justifying them or repeating them. It means learning from them and moving on from them. When you fail, learning from it is key to both doing better in the future and moving beyond the limitations that failure might create. Engaging in sincere introspection is necessary to evaluate your failures thoroughly. When you embrace this process, then will you discover the potential that lies within them. For instance, consider a situation where you undertook a project but didn't achieve the desired outcome. What did you learn from that experience, and how can it help you in the future? Maybe you learned about what not to do as much as you learned what you should do.
- **Accept your flaws and imperfections:** These are the aspects of yourself that you dislike or wish to change. They can be related to your appearance, personality, attitudes, or preferences. Accepting your flaws and imperfections means loving yourself despite them and embracing them as a part of the whole "you." At this stage, many people make the mistake of allowing these flaws to shape their identity. Your flaws don't define you, and they don't invalidate your

inherent worth as a person. You might be a bit overweight, but that doesn't make you a bad person. You might have a big nose, but that doesn't mean you're not attractive. You might want to lose weight or get a nose job, and that's fine because that doesn't define you, either. Your self-worth is something you possess, no matter your imperfections.

Embarking on the path of self-acceptance is a fulfilling voyage that can greatly enrich your life. It nurtures personal growth, propels you toward your aspirations, and enhances your connections with others. Moreover, it empowers you to make a positive impact on the world by sharing your unique gifts, talents, and passions. Remember that you are unique, valuable, and worthy of respect, love, and happiness. You are enough just as you are.

Exercise #2

Finding and Challenging Your Core Beliefs

Core beliefs are sneaky. They hide within our psyche and manipulate our behavior. Negative beliefs are like parasites, latching onto our mindset and leading us astray from our true potential and happiness. But you can expose and challenge those core beliefs, and this is another two-part exercise to do that. The first step will be exposing your core beliefs.

Part 1

Identifying Your Core Beliefs

One way to identify your core beliefs is to practice a meditation exercise that involves self-inquiry and reflection:

1. Find a comfortable and quiet place where you can sit or lie down without distractions. Close your eyes and take 10 deep breaths to relax your body and mind. These breaths should expand both your chest and your stomach.
2. Bring your attention to your heart center: the area in the middle of your chest. Imagine a warm and gentle light in your heart radiating love and compassion. Feel this light expanding and filling your whole being with peace and joy.
3. Ask yourself: What do I believe about myself? What do I believe about others? What do I believe about the world? Listen to the answers that come up in your mind without judging or rejecting them. Just observe them as they are.
4. For each answer, ask yourself: Is this belief true? How do I know it is true? What evidence do I have to support it? How does this belief make me feel? How does this belief affect my actions and decisions? Be honest with and curious about yourself.
5. If you find a belief that is negative, unhelpful, or distorted, ask yourself: Where did this belief

come from? When did I learn it? Who taught it to me? How did it serve me in the past? How is it limiting me now? What would happen if I let go of this belief?
6. If you find a belief that is positive, helpful, or accurate, ask yourself: How can I strengthen this belief? How can I use it to empower myself and others? How can I express it in my life? How can I celebrate it?
7. Once you have explored your core beliefs, thank yourself for doing this exercise and acknowledge your courage and willingness to grow. Redirect your focus to the center of your heart and reconnect with the radiant light residing within. Send some of this light to yourself and anyone or anything you wish to bless. Open your eyes and return to consciousness.

Part 2

Changing Your Core Beliefs

One exercise for challenging and changing negative core beliefs is to use a cognitive restructuring technique called Socratic questioning. Socratic questioning is a method of asking open-ended questions to help you examine your thoughts and beliefs more critically and logically. The goal is to identify and challenge any distortions, errors, or irrationalities in your thinking that may be causing you emotional distress or interfering with your goals.

To use Socratic questioning, you can follow these steps:

1. Identify a negative core belief that you want to change. For example, "I am worthless."
2. Write down any evidence that would support this belief. For example, "I failed an exam," "I got rejected by someone I liked," or "I don't have many friends."
3. Now, write down evidence that contradicts this belief. For example, "I passed other exams before," "There are people who care about me," "I have qualities that I like about myself."
4. Ask yourself questions that challenge the validity, accuracy, and usefulness of your belief. For example, "Is this belief based on facts or feelings?" "Is this belief always true or are there exceptions?" "How does this belief help or hurt me?" and "What would I tell a friend who had this belief?"
5. Based on your answers, come up with a more balanced and realistic alternative belief that takes into account both the positive and negative aspects of yourself and your situation. For example, "I am not worthless; I have strengths and weaknesses like everyone else."
6. Repeat this exercise whenever you become aware of negative core beliefs and wish to replace them with more positive ones through consistent practice.
7. Write down your list of alternative beliefs; every time you notice your negative self-talk kick in,

pull out your list and replace that negative belief with a positive alternative.

Final Thoughts on Core Beliefs

The core beliefs that you've accepted as true often form in an instant. As a child, you pick up offhand comments made by those you love and respect, and you make a judgment about yourself as a result of those comments. At times, such beliefs stem from abusive experiences by a caretaker who, despite intending to act in your best interest, may have been too emotionally wounded to fulfill the role of a nurturing parent. But the core beliefs we adopt are not who we truly are. We are so much more than that, and by identifying and changing your core beliefs, you are acknowledging that fact. You are acknowledging that not only are you not worthless, stupid, unkind, or insensitive; rather, you are beautiful, and you have the capacity to change. By embarking on this journey of healing, you have already demonstrated your remarkable courage. That alone shows you're far more than what you identified with as a frightened and impressionable child. To truly heal those core beliefs, it is crucial to identify the emotional triggers stemming from the wounds we experienced during our early years. That's what the next chapter will explore.

Chapter 3

Identifying Emotional Triggers and Wounds

All of us walk this world wounded. Even those with the brightest of childhoods have had some sort of wound that they carry with them into their adult lives. Although painful when experienced, these wounds serve as profound opportunities for growth. They form part of who we are, and if we live to adulthood, we are, above all else, survivors. That's an incredible and empowering way to look at the wounds you received, no matter how awful they were at the start. Somehow you survived, and doesn't that make you an extraordinary person? I think it does, and when you learn to recognize that too, you can then defuse your triggers and heal those wounds. You can become the superhero you have always wanted to become. You can replace outdated behaviors with healthier coping mechanisms that foster personal growth. The process begins with understanding what the emotional triggers represent and identifying yours.

What Triggers You?

Emotional triggers are stimuli that evoke strong emotional reactions in us like anger, fear, sadness, or joy. They can be external, such as words, actions, or events, or internal, such as memories, thoughts, or feelings. Emotional triggers stem from intense, traumatic, or recurring past experiences and associations. They can affect our behavior in various ways, depending on how we cope with them.

Some examples of emotional triggers include:

- Hearing a song that reminds us of a happy or painful memory.
- Seeing a familiar face of someone who hurt or helped us.
- Smelling a scent that brings back a memory of a place or person.
- Feeling a physical sensation tied to an emotion, such as a tight chest or a warm hug.
- Reading or watching something that resonates with our values or beliefs.

When triggered, we may subconsciously react without awareness of the underlying cause. This can lead to impulsive, irrational, harmful, or otherwise inappropriate behavior. For example, we may lash out at someone who says something that reminds us of a past insult, or we may avoid a situation that makes us feel anxious or vulnerable. The alternative is that we respond consciously and intentionally by recognizing and regulating our emotions and choosing how to act accordingly. This can lead to adaptive, rational, and more appropriate behavior that may benefit ourselves or others. For example, we may use humor to diffuse a tense situation or seek support from someone who understands us. Emotional triggers can be an opportunity for growth and healing if we learn how to identify and cope with them effectively. Becoming more aware of our emotional triggers and their origins enhances our self-understanding and empathy toward others. Additionally, as we develop healthy coping skills and strategies to manage these triggers, we can minimize their negative effects and foster greater emotional resilience and well-being.

Before we go further, let's take a look at the four levels of emotional reactions that we typically have.

The Four Levels of Emotional Reactions

The four levels of emotional reactions are physiological arousal, cognitive appraisal, subjective experience, and behavioral response. These four levels form a cycle of emotion, and understanding each one can help us better recognize our own emotional reactions and the emotions of others.

1. Physiological Arousal
2. Cognitive Appraisal
3. Subjective Experience
4. Behavioral Response

The first level is that of physiological arousal, which is the physical response we experience when our body reacts to a particular emotion. This could include increased heart rate, and increased breathing, among other physical reactions.

The second level is cognitive appraisal, which is how we interpret our emotions. We consider the context of the emotion and decide whether it's positive or negative. We may also assign a label to the emotion, such as "happy" or "sad."

The third level is subjective experience, which is how we feel the emotion. It encompasses the emotional aspect of our reaction, which we can often articulate using words like "joy" or "anger."

The fourth level is behavioral response, which is how we act on the emotion. This could include verbal or physical reactions, such as shouting or hugging. Understanding these four levels of emotional reactions can enhance our comprehension of both our own emotions and the emotional responses of others. It also aids in improving our emotional management by teaching us to foster self-awareness of our feelings and enabling us to respond more appropriately to different situations.

Four More Levels

According to psychologist Robert Plutchik, emotions can further be categorized into four more levels: primary, secondary, tertiary, and quaternary. Let's explore how these levels reflect different emotional triggers and how they can affect our behavior and well-being.

1. **Primary Emotions:** Primary emotions are the most basic and instinctive ones, such as joy, sadness, anger, fear, surprise, and disgust. They are triggered by events that directly impact our survival, such as threats, losses, or rewards. Primary emotions are universal and innate, meaning that they are shared by all humans and animals, and they do not depend on learning or culture.
2. **Secondary Emotions:** Secondary emotions are more complex and nuanced, examples being guilt, shame, pride, envy, jealousy, and gratitude. They are triggered by events with an indirect impact on our survival, such as social interactions, moral judgments, or self-evaluation. Secondary emotions are influenced by learning and culture, meaning that they vary across individuals and groups and depend primarily on social norms and values.
3. **Tertiary Emotions:** Tertiary emotions are even more complex and subtle than secondary emotions. They include emotions like awe,

wonder, curiosity, boredom, anticipation, and disappointment and are triggered by events with no immediate impact on our survival; rather, they have to do with our cognitive and aesthetic interests. Tertiary emotions are driven by learning and culture, meaning they depend on our knowledge and preferences while reflecting our goals and motivations.

4. **Quaternary Emotions:** Quaternary emotions are the most complex and refined of the four types and include emotions such as compassion, empathy, sympathy, love, hate, and contempt. They are triggered by events that involve other people's emotions or perspectives. Quaternary emotions are based on learning and culture, meaning they require a high level of cognitive and social skills and express our moral and ethical values.

These levels reflect different aspects of our human nature and experience. Understanding them can help us regulate our emotions better and improve our relationship with ourselves and others.

The Importance of Identifying and Defusing Emotional Triggers

I remember that on one of my very first dates, my date made a very casual remark about the dress I was wearing. It wasn't intended as an insult, and in fact, he meant it as a compliment, but the way he said it triggered intense shame in me. I recall experiencing an overwhelming surge of shame and self-blame, accompanied by a flood of emotions and thoughts. I was fully triggered. Needless to say, the date didn't last very long, but my shame did. I remember trying so hard to understand why I had felt the way I did. I didn't remember a specific incident in my past, and I wasn't consciously aware of any particular wound related to that. My dress wasn't risque; it just looked nice on me. That was my intention for the date, yet, inexplicably, I emerged from the experience feeling dirty. It took me a considerable amount of time to comprehend the origin of those unsettling feelings and the underlying reason for believing that I had let someone down in some way. This is how an emotional trigger sneaks into our lived experiences. Unrelated actions or circumstances can unexpectedly evoke a strong response, even if they have no direct connection to the original source of your emotional trigger. A passing comment, a scent, a color, a taste, or various other stimuli may have the power to elicit such intense reactions. Emotional triggers stem from past experiences, including trauma, abuse, neglect, or loss, which have imprinted lasting impressions on our psyche. Encountering a trigger can lead to disproportionate or harmful reactions that extend beyond the present situation, impacting both ourselves and others. For example, we may lash out at our partner for being late because it reminds us of a time when we felt abandoned by someone we loved. Or, as in my case, we may shame ourselves ruthlessly due to our negative core beliefs.

Identifying and defusing emotional triggers is becoming more aware of our feelings and reactions and learning to cope with them healthily. Recognizing triggers involves identifying physical sensations, thoughts, or behaviors, understanding their source in memories, beliefs, or needs, and finding soothing and calming techniques like breathing exercises, meditation, or self-compassion. By doing this, we can reduce the intensity and frequency of our emotional reactions and prevent them from escalating into conflicts or crises.

Healing the wounds that created these triggers involves a thorough and ongoing process of addressing the underlying issues that have caused us pain and distress. It involves exploring our past experiences and how they have shaped us, acknowledging and expressing our emotions and needs, challenging and changing our negative beliefs and patterns, and seeking support and guidance from others who can help us heal. By doing this, we can gradually heal our wounds and develop a more positive and resilient sense of self.

How Can Toxic People Use Emotional Triggers to Control Us?

Toxic people are those who manipulate, abuse, or harm others for their own benefit. Narcissists are an example of a toxic personality type. They often use our emotional triggers to control us and make us feel guilty, ashamed, or angry. Because emotional triggers evoke strong reactions in us, toxic people are able to easily utilize them to gain control and manipulate others. Toxic people, like my mother, spend the early stages of a relationship getting to know you in order to recognize your emotional triggers. Then, they use manipulation techniques to trigger you. Most people use this kind of manipulation without realizing they're doing it. They may have learned it from their parents or experiences, and it worked for them. But some people, like psychopaths and narcissists, will use these techniques consciously, or at least semi-consciously. They purposefully trigger you so they can then manipulate you.

One way that toxic people can use our emotional triggers is by gaslighting. This was a favorite tactic of my mother; she loved to make me question my reality. If I had a need, I was selfish, and if I wanted to do something that any young kid would want to do, I was lazy. That's what gaslighting is; it's a form of psychological abuse where the abuser makes the victim doubt their memory or perception. For example, a toxic partner may deny that they cheated on their spouse, even when there is clear evidence of their infidelity. They may even accuse their spouse of being paranoid, crazy, or insecure. They may also twist the facts or lie to make their spouse feel confused or guilty. By doing this, they are using the spouse's emotional trigger of insecurity or betrayal to make them question their sanity and judgment. My narcissistic ex-husband used this tactic frequently and was very skilled at twisting any argument we had into being my fault. My own codependency played a role in this abuse too. I felt like I needed him, and I desperately wanted to please him—and I questioned whether I was being unreasonable. He was so certain that I was, and since I was isolated from my friends and family members, I had no one to turn to for another perspective. When someone is successful at this technique, their victim will believe they have to rely on the toxic individual for a proper interpretation of reality.

Another way that toxic people can use our emotional triggers to control us is by projecting. Projecting is a defense mechanism where the person attributes their own negative feelings or traits onto someone else. For example, a toxic boss may blame their employees for their own mistakes or failures. They may criticize their employees for being lazy, incompetent, or dishonest and may also accuse them of having ulterior motives or hidden agendas. By doing this, they are using the employees' emotional triggers of fear or anxiety to make them feel inferior or unworthy. Narcissists often accuse others of being narcissistic, particularly when they can steal the spotlight away from the narcissist. This is a classic example of projecting; they are projecting their own toxic traits onto their victims. Oftentimes, the victims are so confused that they begin to believe the projection.

A third way that toxic people can use our emotional triggers is for triangulating. Triangulating is a manipulation tactic where the person creates conflict or drama between two or more people. For example, they may gossip about one friend to another, spreading rumors, lies, or secrets that could cause mistrust or jealousy between those two friends. They may also play the victim or hero in different situations to gain sympathy or admiration from others. By doing this, they are using the friends' emotional triggers of anger or envy to make them fight with each other. Narcissists often use triangulation to create an atmosphere of mistrust between family members. They don't want their victims to be close enough to anyone else in the family to figure out what they're doing. In this way, you believe you don't have anyone you can turn to for another point of view.

Toxic individuals have the ability to inflict significant harm by exploiting our emotional triggers, and manipulating us psychologically. Therefore, it is crucial to identify and neutralize our own triggers, ensuring that they cannot be weaponized against us by anyone. The truth is that you should be able to be vulnerable with the person you love. You should be able to show them your wounds and trust that they won't use them against you. But so many people have damaged themselves, and that person could use what they learned about you to manipulate and further abuse you. When you defuse that trigger and heal that old wound, you take away that weapon. You take back control over your own emotional responses, and you can be vulnerable without exposing yourself to manipulation and abuse.

We tend to mistake our stories for our identity, but they are not one and the same. Your story is simply something that happened to you; it's not who you are. Who you are is so much more profound than any one story from your life. It's common to get caught up in the narratives our minds create, which can lead us to be carried away by our emotions. When you realize that the story is just that: a story, then can you let it go. You can let it be a part of your life without making it a part of your identity. Then you can really see the gifts that the story has given you and how it has made you stronger.

Codependency and Emotional Triggers

Codependent people are especially vulnerable to emotional triggers because they have learned to suppress their 1 needs and feelings to please others. Codependency is a dysfunctional relationship pattern that often develops in childhood when caregivers are emotionally unavailable, abusive, or neglectful. Codependent people grow up feeling insecure, unworthy, and afraid of abandonment. They seek validation and self-worth from external sources, such as their partners, friends, or family members, and develop patterns of behavior that allow them to love themselves through other people's love for them. In my own situation, I wanted to please the people in my life so they would love me, and when they loved me for all I was doing for them, I was, in that sense, loving myself. But to get that sensation, I put everyone else's needs above my own, neglecting my own needs and desires. I suppressed what I wanted because I so desperately needed the other person to love me and see my worth. My childhood experiences left me with very low self-esteem. It didn't feel like I was enough, but if I could just do enough for other people, and they loved me for that, then I could feel worthy of love. You can probably see how this set me up for emotional abuse and control.

Emotional triggers can be used to manipulate codependent people by exploiting their fears and insecurities. For example, someone may accuse their codependent partner of being selfish or too sensitive when they express their opinions or desires. This can trigger guilt, shame, and self-doubt in the codependent person, who may then apologize and comply with their partner's wishes. This often happened with my narcissistic ex. Alternatively, the individual may use threats of leaving or ignoring their codependent partner as a means to discourage the partner from establishing boundaries or asserting their needs. This can trigger anxiety, panic, and abandonment in the codependent person, who may then beg for forgiveness and cling to the partner.

It's easy for some toxic people to identify your weaknesses. They may recognize that you fear abandonment, perhaps because you told them in the earlier idealization stage of your relationship. Narcissists, for example, will use that early period to be as charming as they can possibly be. It is believed that many romantic partners of narcissists meet their "soulmates" during this early stage. Narcissists are extremely charming at this point in the relationship, but they can't maintain that facade for long. That's why they learn everything they can about you in that early stage. Even when they seem ever so charming, they are actually gathering ammunition to use against you. They learn about your vulnerabilities, old wounds, and emotional triggers. Then, they can discern how to use them against you.

Emotional manipulation can have harmful effects on codependent people's mental and physical health. It can erode their self-esteem, identity, and autonomy. It can also cause them to experience chronic stress, depression, anxiety, and other psychological problems. Moreover, emotional manipulation can prevent codependent people from developing healthy and interdependent relationships with others.

After leaving my narcissistic ex, I was extremely depressed. I experienced deep feelings of loneliness and a lack of love. What's worse, I believed that I didn't deserve love. This is codependency. The toxic person wants someone with this kind of behavioral pattern to feel this exactly. Had I not recognized that something was wrong with me and pursued a journey of healing, I might have gone running back to my narcissistic ex, pleading for his forgiveness. Many codependent people do just that—and there were certainly times in my life when I had reacted very similarly. But you can break free of that kind of control. Codependent people can overcome emotional manipulation by becoming aware of their triggers and how those triggers affect behavior. They can also learn to recognize the signs of manipulation and set boundaries with their partners. So how can you recognize and defuse your emotional triggers? Let's take a look.

Exercise #3

Trigger Warning

Recognizing, defusing, and healing emotional triggers consists of two essential components. The first part revolves around identifying and diffusing the triggers themselves. The second part focuses on actively addressing and healing the original wound that gave rise to the trigger.

Part 1

Identifying Your Triggers

Identifying our emotional triggers can help us understand ourselves better and cope with difficult emotions more effectively. Here are the steps to take when identifying your emotional triggers:

1. **Reflect on your past experiences:** When you have a quiet moment where you can reflect without interruption, engage in uninterrupted reflection. Find a peaceful space, sit quietly, and delve into moments when you experienced intense emotions, be it positive or negative. It can be something recent or something that happened a long time ago.
2. **Tell the story:** What was the situation? Who was involved? What did you say or do? How did you feel afterward? Recall as many details as possible and write them down in a journal.
3. **Look for patterns:** After reflecting on several situations where you had a strong emotional response over the course of a week or two, review your journal entries and see if you can find any common triggering themes. For example, you might notice that you tend to feel angry when someone criticizes you, or maybe you feel happy when you receive praise or appreciation. You might also notice that certain people, places, or topics tend to trigger your emotions more often than others.
4. **Understand the underlying causes:** Once you have identified those patterns and recognized your emotional triggers, take the opportunity to delve deeper into understanding why they have such a significant impact on you. What's the story you tell yourself when triggered? What beliefs, values, or expectations do you have that

make you react strongly to certain situations? For example, if you feel angry when someone criticizes you, it might be because you believe you need to be perfect or that you are not good enough. If you feel happy when you receive praise or appreciation, it might be because you value recognition or approval from others.

5. **<u>Learn to manage your emotions:</u>** Knowing your emotional triggers can help you prepare for and deal with them more effectively. You can use various strategies to cope with your emotions, such as breathing exercises, relaxation techniques, positive affirmations, cognitive restructuring, or seeking support from others. You can also try to avoid or minimize exposure to your emotional triggers, if possible and appropriate. For example, if you know that a certain person or topic tends to make you angry, you can try to limit your contact with them or change the subject. Try this the next time you feel triggered:

❖ Take 10 deep breaths before responding to the situation. Breathe into both your belly and chest.

❖ After calming yourself with breathing, repeat an appropriate affirmation. For example, if you feel bad because someone criticized you, try repeating the following affirmation: ***I am not my mistake. Like everyone, I am human, and I make mistakes, and I can learn from them. My value as a person is independent of any mistakes I make.***

- Utilize your positive self-talk from Chapter 2. For example, if you did something wrong and your first thought is, "I'm so stupid," stop and use your positive alternative. It might be something like, "I'm glad I made that mistake because now I have learned something new."

Part 2

Healing Those Old Wounds

Identifying your triggers is just the first part of dealing with them. The next step is identifying and healing the old wound that created them. Here's one method you can use to do that.

1. **Reengage with the story:** Sit again in a quiet place where you won't be interrupted. Bring to mind a time when you felt strongly triggered. Replay that situation until you can once again feel the emotions associated with the trigger.
2. **Remember the first time:** Once you're fully engaged with the emotion associated with your trigger, try to remember the first time you felt that way. This may require revisiting events from your distant past, as they are often deeply ingrained in our memories and can be readily recalled.
3. **Look at the situation with different eyes:** When this wound happened, you were someone very different from the person you've become.

You were probably just a child and didn't know how to respond to the situation. View the situation again through your adult eyes. Can you see your little self trying to cope? Can you have compassion and empathy for that child? How should they have been treated?

Now that you are aware of the harm that was inflicted, what actions or steps would you take moving forward? How would you comfort them? Do it now the way it should have been done then.

4. **See the other side:** Turn your attention and insight to the other people in that situation. Can you see the person or people who made you feel bad about yourself? Can you see them through compassionate eyes? Can you see a mother struggling to raise a child by herself or dealing with her own psychological damage? Can you envision a father who grew up in an abusive household and lacks knowledge of effective parenting techniques due to his upbringing? Can you see the damage those people endured in their lives that made them treat you the way they did? For example, in my mother's case, she was dealing with a lot of loss herself. She was also trying to salvage her family in a very dangerous part of the world during an uncertain political time. As I reflect on the instances when she caused me harm, I can see her own desperation and pain. Although that doesn't excuse what she

did—that's not the point—it does help me understand it, and with understanding comes healing.

5. **See the gift:** It's time to see the gift that situation brought you. You survived, so there's a gift there. As a child, you used whatever tactics you could to deal with your pain, and it worked because you survived. Those tactics may not serve you anymore, but they got you through that situation. While my mother encouraged my codependency by expecting me to be a caretaker in the family, in doing so, I became more resilient. I learned how to take care of other people. Granted, I put aside my own needs in doing so, but I still learned some valuable insights that I can still use, even though I now prioritize myself. I learned how to be a good caretaker—that's a valuable skill.

6. **Let the story go:** Now that you've relived this experience, you can finally let the story go. You can let it be just what it was: something that happened to you a long time ago. It no longer defines you; it's just an incident that happened in your life. Thank your little self for being so brave, bless your abuser with compassion, and let the story become just another scene in the movie that is your life.

Final Thoughts on What Triggers You

Emotional triggers and the underlying wounds that created them are ammunition that toxic people can use to control and manipulate us. For codependents, those triggers are often associated with wounds that instill worthlessness and hopelessness. We were made to believe our value was based solely on what we could do for others. The truth is that your value is inherent in your very existence. You bring light to the world and people you love, and now, you can bring it to yourself. It's time to give yourself what you should have received so many years ago. It's time to be the parent you didn't have. You can't change the past, but you can be a kind, loving, giving, and supportive caretaker to yourself going forward. You have the power to heal the child within you who is still carrying the wounds of those past traumas. Let's explore how you can go about doing just that.

Chapter 4

What Your Inner Child Needs

Inside every one of us is the child we once were. There's a little you who endured the wounds of childhood and helped you to survive some very difficult times. Everyone has experienced some kind of trauma in childhood that left scars. Our inner child retains those scars, and sometimes, that little you needs help to overcome those consequences.

The problem is that you can't go back. That's what most people who have suffered childhood trauma, particularly codependent people, are trying to do when they form adult relationships. They're trying to relive those old relationships and make them come out right this time. But that's no longer a possibility. What happened in your childhood is over and done with. Even if the people who abused you acknowledged their abusive behavior and apologized, it wouldn't heal your inner child. The damage is done, but that doesn't mean it can't be healed. You, and only you, hold the key to doing that work, however. You can heal your inner child by being the parent or friend they didn't have the first time around. That's what your inner child needs. They don't need your abusive mother, father, or whoever hurt you in your life to accept and love them; they need you to accept and love them. But before you can do that, you need to understand a little more about who your inner child really is and what they mean to you now, as an adult.

What is the Concept of the Inner Child?

The concept of the inner child refers to the psychological idea that within us exists a part of our personality that retains the qualities and characteristics of our childhood self. The inner child is often associated with creativity, spontaneity, curiosity, playfulness, and emotional expression. However, the inner child can also carry the wounds, traumas, and negative beliefs that we experienced as children. These can affect our adult behavior, relationships, and well-being.

According to some psychotherapists, such as John Bradshaw, Eric Berne, and Alice Miller, healing the inner child is an essential step in overcoming emotional problems and achieving personal growth. They suggest that by reconnecting with our inner child, we can access the positive qualities that we may have lost or suppressed while also healing the pain from our past. Some benefits of healing the inner child include:

- Increased self-esteem and self-acceptance
- Reduced anxiety and depression
- Enhanced creativity and joy
- Improved communication and intimacy
- Greater resilience and coping skills

Without healing your inner child, you may continue to live through old patterns of behavior. You might also find it difficult to overcome your struggles due to using unhelpful coping strategies.

How Does Our Inner Child Affect Our Behavior?

Our inner child is the part of us that retains the memories, emotions, and beliefs we formed in our early years. It is the source of our creativity, joy, and curiosity, but it is also of our fears, insecurities, and wounds. Our inner child plays a significant role in shaping our behavior, influencing us both positively and negatively. One of the main ways that our inner child affects our behavior is through our relationships with others. Our inner child shapes our attachment style and what we expect from others, which is how we relate to the latter emotionally. Depending on our childhood experiences, we may develop a secure, anxious, avoidant, or disorganized attachment style.

A secure attachment style means we trust others, feel comfortable with intimacy and independence, and have a positive view of ourselves and others. An anxious attachment style means we crave closeness and approval from others, are afraid of abandonment and rejection, and view ourselves and others negatively. An avoidant attachment style means we value independence and autonomy over intimacy and connection, avoid emotional involvement and commitment, and have a negative view of others while having a positive view of ourselves. A disorganized attachment style means that we have contradictory and inconsistent behaviors and expectations in relationships, experience confusion and fear around intimacy and trust, and view ourselves and others negatively.

Our attachment style affects how we communicate, express our needs and emotions, handle conflicts, and support our partners. For example, someone with an anxious attachment style may be clingy, needy, jealous, or controlling in a relationship, whereas someone with an avoidant attachment style may be distant, aloof, dismissive, or emotionally unavailable. Someone with a secure attachment style may be able to balance their own needs and emotions with those of their partner, whereas someone with a disorganized attachment style may have difficulty regulating their emotions and maintaining a stable relationship.

Another way that our inner child affects our behavior is through our self-esteem. Our self-esteem, which encompasses how we perceive our own value and assess our worthiness, is strongly influenced by the messages we received from our parents or caregivers during our childhood. If we received unconditional love, acceptance, praise, and encouragement from our parents or caregivers, we are more likely to develop healthy self-esteem. If we received criticism, rejection, neglect, or abuse from our parents or caregivers, we are more likely to develop low self-esteem. Our self-esteem affects how we perceive ourselves and behave in different situations. For example, someone with a healthy self-esteem may have confidence in their abilities and potential, take risks and challenges positively, accept compliments graciously, and cope with failures constructively. Someone with a low self-esteem may doubt their abilities and potential, avoid risks and challenges, reject compliments defensively, and dwell on failures.

A third way that our inner child affects our behavior is through our coping strategies. Our coping strategies refer to the methods we employ to navigate and manage stressors and challenges in life, and these strategies are shaped by the coping skills we learned from our parents or caregivers during our formative years. If we learned healthy coping skills from our parents or caregivers, we may develop more adaptive coping strategies. If we learned unhealthy coping skills, we may develop maladaptive coping strategies. Adaptive coping strategies help us reduce stress, resolve problems, and enhance well-being; on the other hand, maladaptive coping strategies increase stress, cause us to avoid problems, and impair our well-being. Some examples of adaptive coping strategies include seeking social support, practicing relaxation techniques, engaging in hobbies or interests, and expressing emotions appropriately. Examples of maladaptive coping strategies include isolating oneself, substance abuse or addictive behaviors, suppressing or denying emotions, and blaming yourself or others. Our coping strategies play a significant role in determining our responses to difficulties and our level of resilience in overcoming them. For instance, individuals with adaptive coping strategies often approach challenges with optimism and resourcefulness, enabling them to navigate difficulties effectively. Conversely, those with maladaptive coping strategies may feel overwhelmed by challenges, leading to pessimism and helplessness.

Our inner child influences our relationships, our self-esteem, and our coping strategies. By becoming aware of and healing our inner child, we can improve our behavior. We have the capacity to develop and embrace more effective coping strategies that empower us to navigate life's challenges. By enhancing our self-esteem and acknowledging our intrinsic worth, we can forge healthier connections with our loved ones and realize that our self-love is not contingent upon external validation. Nurturing self-compassion and self-love enables us to extend compassion and love to others as well. Those are the benefits of healing your inner child, but how do you go about doing that?

Healing Your Inner Child

There are many directions we can take to heal our inner child, depending on our needs and preferences. Some common methods include:

1. **Inner child work:** This is identifying, acknowledging, and communicating with the inner child through techniques such as journaling, meditation, visualization, art therapy, or role-playing. The goal is to understand the inner child's needs, feelings, and desires and provide them with the love, support, and validation they may have lacked in childhood. With this work, you are building your inner child a new home to live in.
2. **Reparenting:** This is a form of self-care that involves treating yourself like a loving and nurturing parent would treat a child. This means providing yourself with physical, emotional, mental, and spiritual nourishment, such as healthy food, rest, exercise, comfort, affirmation, guidance, and discipline. The aim is to develop a positive and compassionate relationship with yourself and correct negative messages you may have internalized from your parents or caregivers.
3. **Therapy:** This is a professional intervention that can help you explore and resolve issues that stemmed from your childhood experiences. A therapist can help you identify and challenge the

dysfunctional patterns you may have learned from your family, such as codependency, abuse, neglect, or abandonment. A therapist can also help you process and release any emotions you may have repressed or denied.

Healing the inner child is not necessarily a quick or easy process. It requires courage, patience, and commitment. However, it can also be rewarding and transformative. By healing the inner child, you can reclaim your true self and live a more authentic and fulfilling life.

Building a New Home for Your Inner Child

The journey of healing and growth involves constructing a renewed inner core for your inner child, enabling you to transcend past wounds and embrace your true and authentic self. Your inner child is the part of you that holds your childhood memories, emotions, and needs, both positive and negative. Sometimes, your inner child may feel hurt, scared, angry, or ashamed due to your memories and experiences. This can affect how you relate to yourself and others in the present.

To build a new inner core for your inner child, you need to acknowledge, validate, and soothe your inner child's feelings, as well as challenge and change any limiting beliefs or fears that hold you back. Here are some basic steps to help you accomplish this:

1. **Acknowledge your inner child:** Recognize that you have an inner child who needs your attention and care. You can do this by closing your eyes and imagining yourself as a child at different ages. Notice how you look, what you wear, how you feel, and what you need. What do you see when you look back on your life at different stages?
2. **Validate your inner child's feelings:** Listen to what your inner child is telling you through your emotions, sensations, thoughts, and behaviors. Don't judge, criticize, or dismiss their feelings; instead, empathize with and reassure them that they are normal, natural, and understandable. Your inner child is screaming out for your attention—don't push them away. Rather than dismissing them, lend an ear and listen to their messages. They yearn to express their needs: the unmet desires from long ago that still resonate within you.
3. **Soothe your inner child:** Offer comfort and support to your inner child when they are in distress. You can do this by hugging yourself, rocking yourself, breathing deeply, meditating, playing soothing music, or doing anything else that makes you feel calm and safe. You are the safe home for your inner child; you just need to help them recognize and know that you are a safe haven in a storm. Let them know that you will always be there for yourself and on your side.

4. **<u>Challenge your inner child's beliefs and fears:</u>** Identify any negative or limiting beliefs or fears that your inner child has developed as a result of your childhood experiences. For instance, you may believe that you are not good enough, worthy of love, safe, or in control. These beliefs and fears may prevent you from living authentically and fulfilling your potential. Challenge those beliefs and fears by telling yourself that you are good enough, worthy, safe, and can always control your own thoughts and emotions. Show your inner child that you are your own hero, and that you will always be there to rescue yourself.

5. **<u>Change your inner child's beliefs and fears</u>**: Replace any negative or limiting beliefs or fears with positive and empowering ones. You can do this by using affirmations, visualizations, journaling, or other techniques that can help you reprogram your subconscious mind. For example, you can say to yourself: "I am good enough," "I am worthy of love," "I am safe," or "I am in control." It also helps to reassure your inner child that the responses you had when you were that little you were perfectly appropriate. It is completely understandable to have felt that way, especially considering the circumstances. Such emotions are valid and natural for a child to experience as well.

6. **Nurture your inner child:** Give your inner child what they need to feel happy, healthy, and fulfilled. You can do this by engaging in activities that bring you joy, creativity, and curiosity and make you playful. You can also express your needs and desires to others and set healthy boundaries. Let your inner child play the way you used to play when you were carefree and exploring your world for the first time.

By nurturing a new inner core for your inner child, you embark on a transformative journey of healing and self-discovery. This process allows you to heal from past wounds, embrace your authentic self, and cultivate a strong sense of self-worth. Through this journey, you can enhance your self-esteem, develop greater self-compassion, boost your self-confidence, and unlock your unique self-expression. Moreover, as you deepen your relationship with yourself, meaningful connections with others will flourish, leading to more fulfilling and authentic relationships. Ultimately, this inner work empowers you to live a life aligned with your true purpose and unleash your full potential.

With the basic concepts in mind, we will now explore some guided exercises to help you build that new core.

Exercise #4

You and Your Inner Child

This exercise will be focused on helping you to reach out to your inner child to better understand the damage they suffered and how you can help them going forward. One of the ways to heal your inner child is to practice a meditative exercise that allows you to connect with your younger self. After you are able to do that successfully, you can progress to healing the pain your inner child suffered with past trauma.

Part 1

Finding Your Inner Child

This exercise will help you to reach out and connect to your inner child. Here are the steps to follow:

1. Find a comfortable and quiet place where you can sit or lie down. Close your eyes and take a few deep breaths to relax your body and mind. Make sure your breaths expand both your belly and your chest.
2. Imagine that you are in a safe and beautiful place, such as a garden, beach, or forest. Feel the warmth of the sun, the breeze of the wind, or the sound of the water. This is your inner sanctuary, where you can meet your inner child.

3. As you explore your inner sanctuary, look for a sign that indicates where your inner child is. It could be a toy, drawing, or symbol. Follow the sign until you find your inner child.
4. Greet your inner child with love and compassion. Notice how they look, what they are wearing, and how they feel. Ask them if they want to talk to or play with you. Respect their wishes and boundaries.
5. Spend some time with your inner child, listening to their stories, feelings, and needs. Validate their emotions and experiences. Tell them that you understand exactly why they feel the way they do and that you are here for them, love them, and are proud of them.
6. When ready, give your inner child a hug and thank them for spending time with you. Tell them that you will come back whenever they need you, will always be on their side, and will always take care of them. Say goodbye and leave them in their safe place.
7. Return to your present awareness by taking a few deep breaths and opening your eyes. Notice how you feel after doing this exercise. Write down any insights or messages that you received from your inner child.

Part 2

Healing Your Inner Child

This exercise can assist you in letting go of any negative emotions, beliefs, or memories that are hindering your ability to reach your full potential. One way to heal the trauma your inner child suffered is to practice a meditative exercise that will connect you with your younger self and offer them compassion and support. This will involve reliving past trauma, so approach this exercise with self-compassion and allow yourself to sit with any of the emotions that arise.

Below is a straightforward step-by-step guide to performing this exercise:

1. **Once more, locate a serene and cozy environment where you can comfortably sit or lie down and unwind:** Close your eyes and take deep breaths, expanding your belly and chest to calm your mind and body.
2. **Imagine you are in that same safe and beautiful place where you first connected with your inner child:** Feel the warmth of the sun, the breeze of the wind, or the sound of the water. This is where you will be meeting them once again.
3. **Call your attention to a past trauma you experienced as a child and visualize your inner child as they were at that time and**

whatever age they were. Notice their appearance, expression, emotions, and needs. How do they feel? What do they want to tell you?

4. **Approach your inner child with kindness and gentleness:** Tell them you are here to listen to, comfort, and help them heal. Ask if they would like a hug or touch from you. Respect their boundaries and preferences.

5. **Take the time to listen to your inner child, validating their feelings and experiences:** Give acknowledgment to their pain and suffering and offer apologies for any neglect or abandonment they may have experienced in the past. Express your unconditional love for them and let them know how proud you are of their resilience in surviving the trauma.

6. **Ask your inner child what they need from you now:** Do they need reassurance, protection, guidance, or encouragement? Do they need you to take any action on their behalf? Do they need you to forgive yourself or someone else? Do whatever you can to meet their needs and honor their wishes. The more you can honor their wishes, the better you will be at healing that old trauma.

7. **Thank your inner child for trusting and sharing with you:** Tell them you will always be there for them and that they can come back to this place anytime they want. Reassure them that

now that the two of you are fully connected, you will listen to them and respect their needs. Give them another hug or touch if they want it, then gently let them go and return to the present moment.

8. **<u>Open your eyes and take a moment to notice how you feel after doing this exercise:</u>** You may feel more peaceful, compassionate, empowered, or healed. You may also feel some emotions or sensations that need further attention or processing. These can sometimes be extremely painful, but if you allow yourself to sit with the pain and process it, you will notice it changing and dissipating. Don't be afraid to let yourself fully feel whatever arises for you. Whatever you are feeling, accept it without judgment and take care of yourself.

Final Thoughts on Your Inner Child

With a strong connection to your inner child, you will develop a heightened awareness of their needs—don't ignore those. Responding to the needs of your inner child will help them heal. By prioritizing your own needs and demonstrating self-care, you will experience accelerated progress in your healing journey, surpassing what would be possible otherwise. This is what most codependent people have found lacking in their lives. They wanted someone to care about them, but what they really needed was to care about themselves. When you prove to yourself that you will always show up for what you need, you will find that you are ready to embrace all parts of yourself—even those you might find disagreeable.

Chapter 5

Embrace Your Shadow Self

Have you ever met someone that you just disliked instantly? Maybe you didn't like the way they dressed, or perhaps their conduct rubbed you the wrong way. Do you remember the intensity of your dislike? Often, this can be a very strong feeling. I know I've met a few people like that in my life. I even speculated that maybe they had murdered me in a previous life. As I embarked on my personal growth journey, I gained a deeper understanding that the intensity of our dislike toward others often stems from the fear of resemblances between them and ourselves. They are exhibiting some traits that we reject in ourselves. When we see someone acting particularly "bad" or "evil" based on our criteria, we react intensely toward that person; however, we are really just judging what we fear is our own shadow self. To heal and become whole, we must understand and embrace our shadow self. Not only is it an important part of our psyche, but our shadow self also brings us gifts to help us thrive. But what exactly do we mean by the "shadow self?"

What is a Shadow Self?

The shadow self is a term coined by <u>Swiss psychologist Carl Jung</u> to describe the hidden aspects of our personality that we tend to repress or deny. It can contain both positive and negative traits, including creativity, anger, sexuality, fear, envy, etc., and is not inherently bad or evil; rather, it is a source of potential that we can integrate into our conscious awareness. According to Jung, the shadow self is formed in childhood as a result of social conditioning and personal experiences. Through social conditioning, we identify the aspects of ourselves deemed acceptable and valued by others, while simultaneously rejecting those that are not. That makes sense from the perspective of a social species that must learn how to behave in a group setting. But by repressing what is considered bad or unacceptable, we often create problems for ourselves that manifest in our subconscious attitudes and actions.

The rejected aspects of ourselves are pushed into the unconscious, where they hide in the shadows and thus, form the shadow self. The shadow self can influence our thoughts, feelings, and behaviors in ways that we are unaware of, often causing problems and conflicts in our lives. Jung believed that the shadow self can be accessed through dreams, fantasies, art, and other forms of expression. He also advocated for a process of individuation, which involves confronting and accepting our shadow self as part of our wholeness. By doing so, we can gain a deeper understanding of ourselves and others and unleash our creative potential. The shadow self is not something to be feared or avoided; rather, it is a challenge and opportunity for personal growth. Let's look a little more closely at just how this side of yourself forms.

How Does Your Shadow Form?

The shadow self contains all the traits, emotions, thoughts, and impulses that we consider unacceptable, immoral, shameful, or negative. For example, if we believe that being angry is bad, we might suppress our anger and eventually project it onto others. If we think being selfish is wrong, we might hide our needs and desires while resenting those who express theirs. The shadow self forms as a result of our socialization and upbringing. From an early age, we learn what is acceptable and what is not in our family, culture, religion, and society. We internalize these norms and try to conform to them in order to gain approval, love, and belonging. However, this also means we have to repress or disown parts of ourselves that do not fit into these expectations. These parts become our shadow self, which remains hidden in our unconscious mind.

The shadow self can manifest in various ways:

Projection

We attribute our negative qualities or feelings to others without realizing they are actually reflections of ourselves. We might accuse someone of being dishonest when *we* are already lying to ourselves.

Compensation

We overemphasize or exaggerate certain positive qualities or behaviors to cover up or balance out our shadow self. We might act overly generous or altruistic when we are secretly feeling greedy or selfish.

Reaction formation

We express the opposite of what we really feel or think, usually in an exaggerated or extreme way. For example, we might act overly friendly or polite when we actually dislike or resent someone.

Repression

We push down or ignore our shadow self, pretending that it does not exist or that it does not affect us. We might deny having any negative feelings or thoughts, even when they are obvious to others.

The shadow self can cause us various problems as well:

1. **Inner conflict:** We feel torn between our conscious self and our shadow self, which brings

us anxiety, guilt, shame, confusion, or dissatisfaction.
2. **Self-sabotage:** Our hidden fears, doubts, or insecurities often manifest unconsciously, leading us to undermine our goals, relationships, or well-being through our actions.
3. **Projection:** We blame others for our own faults or mistakes, creating resentment, hostility, or misunderstanding.
4. **Disconnection:** We lose touch with our authentic self and true potential because we are afraid to face or embrace our shadow self.

Why Should We Integrate the Shadow Self?

The shadow self can also be a source of growth, creativity, and transformation. By becoming aware of and integrating our shadow self, we can achieve wholeness. We can accept and embrace all parts of ourselves, both light and dark, fostering harmony, balance, and peace within ourselves. We also increase self-awareness, helping us gain a deeper understanding of ourselves and recognize our strengths and weaknesses. This self-awareness empowers us to make improvements and learn valuable lessons from our mistakes.

This kind of work allows us to enhance relationships. Through this process, we develop an appreciation for both the differences and similarities among individuals, nurturing trust, respect, and intimacy. Furthermore, as we acknowledge our own needs and prioritize self-care, our relationships with others can be positively influenced. This work also has the potential to unlock creativity by tapping into our hidden talents and passions, enabling us to freely and authentically express ourselves. The result is a life enriched by self-expression and the ability to inspire others.

To integrate our shadow self, we need to:

1. **Acknowledge its existence:** We admit that we have a shadow self and that it influences us in various ways.
2. **Explore its contents:** We examine the traits, emotions, thoughts, and impulses that make up our shadow self and where they come from.
3. **Understand its purpose:** We realize our shadow self is not evil or bad; rather, it is a natural and necessary part of ourselves.
4. **Accept its value:** We appreciate that our shadow self has something to teach and offer us if we listen to and learn from it.
5. **Express its energy:** We find healthy and constructive ways to channel our shadow self into creative outlets or positive actions.

Some examples of what it looks like when you integrate your shadow self include the following:

- A person who represses their anger can learn to assert themselves more effectively and stand up

for their rights without being aggressive or violent. They can learn that it's okay to be angry, and they can learn healthy, constructive ways to express that anger.
- A person who compensates for their insecurity by being arrogant or boastful can learn to be more humble and confident without being self-centered. Through this process, individuals are empowered to assess their strengths and weaknesses with a greater sense of honesty, recognizing that their weaknesses do not define their entire identity. Moreover, they can proactively seek ways to enhance areas in which they desire improvement.
- In their pursuit of self-love, individuals who experience codependency may often suppress their own needs. However, they have the opportunity to cultivate self-love by redirecting their focus inward and prioritizing their own needs as a genuine expression of that love. Doing so will help them develop stronger, healthier, more compassionate, and more loving relationships with other people in their life.

By integrating the shadow self, we can achieve a more balanced and authentic sense of who we are and what we want in life. The benefits of this integration include the following.

It Improves All of Our Relationships

Integrating the shadow self can improve our relationships with others and ourselves. By acknowledging and owning up to our shadow traits, we reduce the tendency to blame, judge, or criticize others for what we dislike in ourselves. We can also develop more empathy and compassion for others who struggle with similar issues. Moreover, we increase our self-esteem by embracing all parts of ourselves—not just the ones we deem acceptable or desirable.

It Enhances Our Personal Growth and Development

Another benefit of integration is that it can enhance our personal growth and development. By exploring and understanding our shadow traits, we can discover new aspects of ourselves that we may have neglected or suppressed. We can also learn from our mistakes and challenges and use them as opportunities for growth and transformation. Furthermore, we can unleash our creative potential and express ourselves more fully and authentically.

It Improves Our Overall Well-Being and Happiness

Integrating the shadow elements of our psyche increases our psychological well-being and happiness. By embracing our shadow self, we alleviate the inner conflict and tension that emerges from denying or disregarding aspects of ourselves. We can also liberate ourselves from the fear of being exposed or rejected by others due to us just being ourselves. Additionally, we can align our actions and values with our true selves, empowering us to pursue our goals and dreams with heightened confidence and passion.

You have to know that integrating the shadow self is not an easy or quick process: it requires courage, honesty, and a willingness to face our dark side and embrace it with love and compassion. However, it is a worthwhile and rewarding journey that can help us become more whole, mature, and fulfilled human beings. It can be difficult, but it is, in the end, a fulfilling one.

How Can We Integrate Our Shadow Self?

The shadow self is not inherently bad or evil; it is simply a part of our wholeness that we have not integrated into our conscious awareness, and it can also contain positive qualities that we have neglected or undervalued, such as creativity, spontaneity or intuition.

Integrating the shadow self is becoming more aware of and accepting the parts of ourselves that we previously rejected or ignored. This can help us achieve greater balance, authenticity, and harmony within ourselves and with others. Incorporating the shadow self can also unleash our hidden potential, allowing us to express ourselves more fully and freely.

There are many ways to integrate the shadow self, but here are some basic concepts that can be helpful for integration:

1. **Identify your shadow self:** The first step is to recognize the signs of your shadow self in your thoughts, feelings, behaviors, and relationships. To achieve this, it would involve acknowledging the triggers, projections, judgments, insecurities, or recurring patterns contributing to your distress or discomfort. Additionally, utilizing techniques like journaling, meditation, dream analysis, or psychological tests can aid in delving into your unconscious mind and revealing hidden aspects of your shadow self. Strong emotional triggers can serve as a valuable signal indicating the presence of your shadow self, which you may unconsciously project into your unconscious mind. Think of it like this: when you push down on dough when making bread, it doesn't disappear; rather, it squishes around your hands and fingers. The shadow does the same thing. You can't banish it from existence—it simply

hides in the darkness, affecting your behavior in the background. Identifying it means finding it in the hidden recesses of your psyche and bringing it into the light.

2. **Acknowledge and accept your shadow self:** The second step is to face your shadow self with honesty and compassion. Instead of denying, avoiding, or resisting your shadow aspects, try to understand and accept them as part of who you are. You can do this by expressing your feelings safely and healthily through writing, talking, or art. You can also practice self-compassion and forgiveness with yourself and others who may have contributed to your shadow formation. Basically, your shadow self wants to step into the light and be seen. By embracing your shadow self with love and acceptance, you unlock the myriad of gifts it holds, even though it may have been hidden until now.

3. **Transform your shadow self:** The third step is to transform your shadow self into a source of strength and growth. Instead of letting your shadow control or limit you, try to learn from and use them for your benefit. You can do this by finding positive ways to channel your shadow energy, such as through creativity, passion, or courage. You can also seek to balance your shadow aspects with their opposite qualities, such as kindness, generosity, or humility. Every shadow brings with it a gift; your selfish shadow

self just wants you to have what you want and need in life. Your greedy shadow self is trying to secure your needs for the rest of your life, and your angry shadow self is expressing a need for a boundary. Within every shadow resides a hidden gift, as each shadow represents a part of yourself that is seeking to assist you in its own unique way. It can help you not just survive, but thrive. By acknowledging this truth, you can embark on a transformative journey where the once-feared shadow evolves from a menacing figure in your nightmares to a heroic presence in your most cherished dreams.

Integrating the shadow self is not a one-time event but a lifelong journey of self-discovery and personal development. There may be many times in your life when you will have to revisit the shadows that have formed in your psyche. It can be challenging and uncomfortable at times—maybe even painful—but it can also be rewarding and liberating. By integrating the shadow self, you become more aware of yourself and others, authentic and confident, compassionate and empathetic, creative and expressive, adaptable and resilient, and whole and complete. Your shadow self is an important part of you, and once you acknowledge and accept its existence, then can you use the gifts it brings to your advantage.

Exercise #5

In the Shadows of Your Mind

One of the most important steps in personal growth is identifying and integrating your shadow self. The first part of this exercise focuses on identifying those shadow elements of yourself. The second part will focus on integrating your shadow selves into the entirety of your identity.

Part 1

You and Your Shadow

To identify your shadow self, you need to be willing to face the parts of yourself that you may not like or accept. A simple exercise to do this is to write down a list of traits you admire or despise in others. For example, you may admire someone's courage, creativity, or generosity, or you may despise someone's arrogance, dishonesty, or selfishness.

Then, for each trait, ask yourself the following questions:

- How does this trait show up in me?
- Do I believe this trait is positive or negative?
- Where did I learn to judge this trait in that way?
- What other characteristics do I associate with this trait?
- How do I express or suppress this trait?

- How does this trait serve or hinder me?

Be honest and compassionate with yourself as you explore these questions. By engaging in this exercise, you acknowledge and embrace your shadow self, leading to a deeper understanding of it and greater self-acceptance. You can harness the power and wisdom of your shadow self instead of fearing or shaming it.

Part 2

Bring Your Shadow into the Light

Integrating the shadow self is becoming more aware, accepting, and compassionate of these aspects of ourselves. Here is a meditative exercise that can help you with this process:

1. Return to that serene and tranquil space where you can comfortably sit or recline. Close your eyes and take 10 deep breaths that expand both your chest and your belly. Relax your body and mind.
2. Bring to your awareness a situation or person that triggers a strong negative emotion in you, such as anger, jealousy, shame, or guilt. Pay attention to the sensations and emotions that arise within your body and mind when you contemplate this situation or person. Take note of where you feel the emotional response and the quality of the sensation that arises.

3. Can you identify a reason for your strong emotional response? Maybe you don't like that they are arrogant because your mother always told you that old Biblical adage, "Pride goeth before a fall." Determine just what creates the strong reaction you feel.
4. Ask yourself: What part of me is being activated by this situation or person? Is this an old wound? Is it part of an internalized belief system? What does this part of me want or need? How does it relate to my shadow self?
5. Visualize a distinct manifestation of this aspect of yourself as if it were standing right in front of you. Observe its appearance, posture, expression, and energy. Can you see that shadow hiding away in a corner of your mind? Try not to judge or criticize it but simply acknowledge its presence.
6. Start a dialogue with this part of you. Ask it questions like: What is your name? What is your purpose? What are you trying to tell me? What do you need from me? Approach this inner entity with a sense of curiosity and openness, listening attentively to its responses. Allow the answers to emerge within you without passing any judgment. Maintain an open mind and a sincere intention to establish a connection with this aspect of yourself.
7. Think honestly about the intentions behind your shadow self. It is possible that this part of

yourself represents suppressed anger or rage. Why is this shadow angry? How does that rage serve you? For example, I struggled with my own shadow self related to anger. My mother had always made it clear that I should never show anger, so I repressed this side of myself. But what does anger give us? Anger serves as a protective tool, helping us set boundaries, meet our needs, and address unfair situations. It can motivate us to take action and promote personal growth when expressed appropriately. Examine the intentions behind your shadow's actions and understand them from the perspective of that part of yourself, acknowledging that it was attempting to serve your best interests.

8. Express your gratitude and appreciation toward this aspect of yourself—its presence and the lessons it has provided. Show appreciation for its role in your growth and healing process. Tell it that you accept it and love it unconditionally and reassure that you understand the intentions behind its influence on your thoughts and behavior. Let it know that you realize it has always been on your side and that you want it to come into the light.

9. Imagine yourself embracing and merging it with your whole being. Feel that wholeness and completeness that arises from integrating your shadow self, and observing any changes in your energy, emotions, or overall well-being. Allow

yourself to fully embody this sense of inner alignment and cherish the newfound harmony within you. I was able to incorporate expressing anger healthily so I could set firm boundaries and prevent further abuse.

10. Once you have embraced your shadow self, bring your attention back to your breaths; take 10 more deep breaths that expand both your belly and chest. As you do so, express love and gratitude for your courage in facing the darkness inside of you and bringing it into the light. Open your eyes and reflect on your experience. Write down any insights or messages you received from your shadow self.

Final Thoughts Up to This Point

With a deeper awareness of the origins of your learned patterns of behaviors, thoughts, and emotions, along with your efforts to heal your inner child and integrate your shadows, you may now be experiencing a range of transformative changes. Do not fear these changes; they are natural and anticipated. Throughout this half of the book, you have engaged in substantial personal growth work. It is likely that you have encountered a multitude of emotions, and it is understandable to feel somewhat disoriented amidst it all. Remember that healing is a gradual process, and it takes time for old wounds to mend completely. This first half of the book has been focused on identifying your patterns of thinking and behavior associated with your codependency. These could have been wounds that created your core beliefs, emotional triggers that formed from your childhood wounds, pain of your inner child, and parts of yourself you relegated to the shadows.

Let yourself experience the changes you're going through and sit with the emotions that come up while continuing to use these techniques to heal. Now it's time to also look at how this process can help you grow into a healthier, happier person. We want to explore how to recognize and prioritize your own needs and why doing so will help make your relationships better. As codependents, we often derive our values from the support we give to other people, but that's a hollow kind of value. True self-value has to come from within—not without. The progress you have made thus far empowers you to embrace these changes and integrate them into your life, fostering personal growth and improvement. You can truly become your own hero—your own Prince or Princess Charming—who will arrive to save the day. When you do, you will discover the beauty of your unique essence, which will be how you create the life you've always dreamed of having.

Chapter 6

Becoming Your Own Hero

What is a hero? This can mean different things to different people. I have a friend who was a teenager in the mid-70s when the movie *Alien*, starring Sigourney Weaver, came out. She was very impressed by this movie because it challenged the stereotype of women in horror movies. Weaver was strong, assertive, and saved herself when no one else could or would. She was not a people-pleaser; she did what needed to be done, and when no one else would listen, she saved herself. In the sequel to that movie, *Aliens*, Weaver revives her role as Ripley and once again plays a stereotype-breaking character as she saves a little girl with the nickname Newt. In one scene, Ripley is holding Newt in her arms as she comes face-to-face with the queen alien creature. It is huge and seems indestructible, but Ripley, though terrified, does not let that stop her, and she ultimately saves them both.

As my friend grew older and began her own healing journey, that's how she envisioned herself in her mind's eye—she was that strong, determined, assertive, and gloriously beautiful woman holding her inner child in her arms as she stood before the seemingly indestructible monsters from her childhood. And she ultimately—same as Ripley—saved them both. You might not be facing a flesh-and-blood, acid-dripping alien from outer space, but your monsters are equally as frightening and may be seemingly as indestructible. Still, you can stand strong with your inner child in your arms and your army of shadow selves as you vanquish them from your lived experience. That's what I call a hero.

Becoming Ripley

Having embarked on the journey of healing your codependency, the next step involves engaging in healthy interactions with others. This entails acquiring the necessary skills to establish boundaries that align with your newfound self-respect and self-love. Embrace the opportunity to fulfill the promise you made to your inner child, becoming the hero they longed for. Let's explore the transformative process of shifting from codependency to independence—from being a people-pleaser to embodying the spirit of Ripley. To begin, we have to recognize what healthy relationships look like; after all, you've been codependent for so long, so it can be difficult to know how to identify emotionally mature ways of interacting with the people you love.

What Exactly is a Healthy Relationship?

A healthy relationship is based on mutual respect, trust, support, and communication. It allows both partners to have their own interests, hobbies, and friends, and both parties should be able to grow as individuals. A healthy relationship does not involve excessive control, manipulation, guilt, or sacrifice. It does not make you feel anxious, frustrated, or pitying of your partner, nor does it mean neglecting your own needs in favor of pleasing others. Interacting with other people is an essential part of human life; however, not all interactions are healthy or beneficial for our well-being. So what exactly characterizes a healthy interaction?

1. **Communication is Key:** It all begins with communication. Healthy interactions with other people require you to communicate clearly and respectfully. This means expressing your thoughts, feelings and needs honestly, politely, and for what is appropriate for the situation. Communication also involves listening actively and empathetically to what others have to say and acknowledging their perspectives and emotions. Active listening means to consider thoughtfully what the other person says. Doing so allows you to see their perspective more clearly. By communicating respectfully, you avoid misunderstandings, conflicts, and hurt

feelings while building trust and rapport with others.

2. **Setting Boundaries is Required:** Another healthy way of interacting with other people is to set boundaries and respect them. Boundaries define the scope of our personal space and the standards we establish for ourselves and others regarding our comfort levels and mutual expectations. They can be physical, emotional, or social and can vary depending on the context and relationship. Setting boundaries helps us protect our personal space, privacy, and autonomy while preventing us from being exploited or manipulated by others. Respecting boundaries means honoring the choices and preferences of others and not imposing your values or expectations on them. Setting boundaries, however, also shows respect for yourself. You are listening to your inner child and respecting your own needs. When you set a boundary with someone else, that's a way of saying that you respect yourself and expect them to do the same.

3. **Giving and Receiving Feedback is Necessary:** A third healthy way of interacting with other people is giving and receiving constructive feedback. Feedback refers to the valuable insights we receive from others regarding our performance or behavior, highlighting areas where we excel or have room for improvement. It can encompass both positive and constructive

aspects, and its effectiveness lies in being specific, relevant, and delivered in a timely manner.

Giving constructive feedback means providing honest and helpful suggestions for improvement without being harsh or judgmental. Receiving constructive feedback means accepting it as an opportunity to learn and grow without becoming defensive or resentful. It can be tricky to accomplish this without offending other people or yourself. The Buddhists say that before saying anything to someone else, you should consider three questions: Is it necessary, is it kind, and is it true? If you can't answer yes to all three, then it's better not to say it. Even if you have to say something that might be negative, you should strive to say it kindly. Others should do the same for you, and if they don't, then you will want to consider carefully their intentions and your relationship with them. Someone who loves and respects you should not want to hurt you.

What About Interacting in Conflicts?

Conflict is inevitable in any relationship, whether it is with a friend, family member, partner, or colleague. However, conflict does not have to be destructive or damaging. In fact, conflict can be an opportunity to learn, grow, and strengthen the bond between two people. The key is to interact healthily during a conflict, which means respecting each other's feelings, needs, and perspectives while avoiding behaviors that can escalate the situation or cause harm.

To avoid that, before engaging in a conflict, take a moment to calm yourself and assess the situation. Ask yourself what the issue is, what you want to achieve from the conversation, and what emotions you are feeling. Doing so can help you avoid reacting impulsively or defensively and prepare you for more constructive dialogue. Use "I" statements instead of "you" statements when expressing your feelings and needs to avoid a "blaming" tone. For example, instead of saying, "You always ignore me when I talk to you," you can say, "I feel hurt when you don't pay attention to me." The other person will become more receptive to your message if you don't make it sound like you're blaming them. Listen actively and empathetically to the other person's point of view and try to understand where they are coming from, what they are feeling, and what they need. Don't interrupt, judge them, or dismiss them; show that you are paying attention by nodding, making eye contact, and paraphrasing what they said.

Another important thing to do is to focus on the problem, not the person. Avoid personal attacks, insults, name-calling, or generalizations. Don't bring up past issues or unrelated topics; stick to the facts and the current situation. Instead of saying, "You're such a lazy and selfish person," you can say, "I'm frustrated that you didn't do your share of the project." Seek to understand before being understood, and don't assume that you know what the other person is thinking or feeling. You never know what may have caused their behavior. Ask open-ended questions to clarify their position and show interest in their perspective. For example, "Can you tell me more about why you did that?" or "How did that make you feel?" might work well. Look for common ground and solutions that benefit both parties rather than viewing the conversation as an opportunity to prove that you are right. Some examples of statements you can try include, "I agree that we both want to do a good job on this project" and "How can we make this work for both of us?"

It's also vital to respect the other person's boundaries and preferences. Give them the freedom to choose when they are ready and comfortable to engage in conversation and avoid placing undue pressure on them to conform to your viewpoint or alter their beliefs. Respect their personal boundaries and refrain from intruding upon their privacy or personal space.

Also respect their right to have different opinions and feelings than yours; it's important to expect them to do the same for you. If they are not doing that, you might need to end the conversation until things have calmed down and everyone can behave respectfully. Of course, you also need to apologize if you hurt or offend the other person. Acknowledge your mistakes and take responsibility for your actions. Express regret and sincerity for what you did or said—you can try these: "I'm sorry for raising my voice at you" or "I apologize for being insensitive to your feelings." When you are respectful to them, it makes it easier to end the conversation on a positive note. Thank the other person for listening and sharing their thoughts with you and express appreciation and gratitude for their efforts and cooperation. Affirm your relationship and commitment to each other with things like "I'm glad we had this talk," "I value our friendship," or "I love you." By expressing appreciation and gratitude, you cultivate a healthy and positive dynamic in your interactions, which has the potential to strengthen both your personal and professional relationships. Moreover, practicing gratitude can contribute to an elevated sense of self-worth and overall happiness. Doing this regularly can help you develop more effective communication, collaboration, and conflict resolution abilities and foster a positive social environment for yourself and others.

Self-Care is Vital for Going from Codependent to Independent

Self-care can help you reduce stress, boost your self-esteem, and increase your independence. It's the one thing that most codependents neglect for themselves; they put other people ahead of their own needs, sometimes to the extent of it being detrimental to their health and well-being.

Self-care practices are essential for maintaining one's physical, mental, and emotional health. They can help reduce stress, improve mood, enhance productivity, and foster resilience. However, many people struggle to find time or motivation to practice self-care regularly. In particular, self-care can boost your immune system and prevent illness. When you take care of your body by eating well, exercising, sleeping enough, and avoiding harmful substances, you are strengthening your natural defenses against infections and diseases. Moreover, practicing self-care can aid in managing chronic conditions such as diabetes, hypertension, or arthritis, allowing you to effectively address symptoms and enhance your overall quality of life.

Another benefit of self-care is that it can improve your mental health and emotional stability. When you take care of your mind by engaging in activities that make you happy, relaxed, and fulfilled, you are reducing stress, anxiety, and depression levels. You are also increasing your self-esteem, confidence, and optimism by acknowledging your strengths and achievements. Furthermore, self-care can help you build healthy relationships with others by enhancing your communication skills, empathy, and compassion.

Here are some of the tips for practicing self-care:

- Set realistic and attainable goals for yourself and celebrate your progress.
- Schedule some time for yourself every day to do something you enjoy or learn something new.
- Seek professional help when you need it and reach out to your support network when you feel lonely or overwhelmed.

- Practice gratitude for what you have and appreciation for those who matter to you.
- Be mindful of your thoughts and feelings and accept them without judgment.
- Practice relaxation techniques such as breathing exercises, meditation, or yoga.
- Say no to things that drain your energy or violate your boundaries.
- Ask for help when you need it and delegate tasks when possible.

It's important to remember that self-care practices are not selfish or indulgent—they are necessary and beneficial for your overall well-being. By taking care of yourself, you are also taking care of others who depend on or care about you. Therefore, make self-care a priority in your life and enjoy the positive outcomes that come with it.

A Word About Seeking Professional Help

If you are struggling with codependency, you may benefit from seeking help from a mental health professional who can provide you with support, guidance, and tools to overcome your challenges. I began my own healing journey this way, and I'm so glad I did. My therapist really helped me see the truth of my codependency and learn how to heal from it. A therapist can help you identify the root causes of your codependency, challenge your negative beliefs and patterns, and teach you new skills and strategies to cope with your emotions and the situation you're in. A therapist can also assist you in establishing objectives for yourself and your relationship, as well as monitoring your advancement and accomplishments.

Seeking out therapy when you need it is not a sign of weakness—it's actually the opposite. It requires courage, commitment, and patience. It also requires a willingness to change yourself and your relationships for the better. To face the demons of your own psyche—the monsters born of childhood trauma—you genuinely have to be a hero. To ask a therapist for help is part of the heroic actions that even Ripley took to deal with the trauma her monsters inflicted. You should not feel even a tinge of shame when you ask for professional help. You should feel proud of yourself for being brave enough to seek out this beneficial form of healthcare.

Another compelling reason to seek professional assistance is that this behavioral pattern often leads to the development of addictions stemming from the prevalent anxiety experienced by codependent individuals. Codependency itself is a type of addiction—an addiction to relationships. Most codependents feel extreme anxiety associated with their fear of losing those they love and the problems that stem from their own low self-esteem. To quell that anxiety, it's not uncommon to turn to substances, food, or behaviors like gambling or excessive use of social media, which would take them away from their inner turmoil. To conquer these addictions, it is crucial to engage the guidance of a professional who can aid you in discovering healthier coping mechanisms and fostering the necessary self-esteem to steer clear of addictive behaviors.

One thing to realize about healing is that it takes time, usually years. It's a long journey, but absolutely worth every second. I remember that many nights as I was going through therapy, I could not sleep. I found myself talking to my mother inside my head as a kid—not as my adult self. I was trying to explain my feelings and blame her for the trauma she inflicted on me. On many occasions, as my wounds healed, I would feel intense pain. I felt anxious and often had destructive thoughts. I even tried to talk to my mom over the phone about what I was going through and my insights. The response? "You've gone crazy with your psychology!"

That's pretty typical. She couldn't understand any of it, and like many perpetrators—who are themselves wounded—she didn't want to understand it. I had to learn to accept her as she was: complete with her current mindset and values. It's hard to feel close to someone with whom you don't share the same values anymore. Grateful for her role as my mother and the gift of life, I appreciate even her devaluation and criticism, recognizing that they have shaped me into the person I am today. With time, I not only forgave her, but I also forgave myself for prioritizing my mother over myself. I created my own inner, supportive, loving mom—the mother I never really had. In doing so, I restored my shine and inner power. It took six years of occasionally excruciating and difficult personal growth work, but I now feel complete within myself. You can achieve this too. Just don't give up; seek out whatever type of care it is you need to reach your potential.

Stop Comparing Yourself to Others

One of the most common sources of unhappiness and stress in our lives, particularly those of us who are codependent, is the habit of comparing ourselves to other people. Whether it's about our appearance, achievements, relationships, or possessions, we often feel inadequate or dissatisfied when we see someone else who seems to have it better than us. But this habit is not only harmful to our mental and emotional well-being—it also prevents us from appreciating and developing our own unique strengths and talents. Comparing ourselves to others can lead to a distorted sense of reality and loss of self-esteem. We may forget that everyone has their own struggles and challenges and that what we see on the surface is not the whole truth. We may also overlook how we are all different and have different goals, values, and preferences. What works for one person may not work for us, and vice versa. By constantly measuring ourselves against others, we are setting ourselves up for disappointment and frustration.

The pervasive comparison culture, fueled by the surge of social media, has reached epidemic proportions. While social media has become deeply ingrained in our lives, its dark side manifests in the form of feelings of inadequacy and unhappiness. Constant exposure to unrealistic standards and idealized portrayals of others' lives on social media contributes to these negative emotions. This phenomenon is known as social comparison, and it can have negative effects on our mental health and well-being. One definition of social comparison is the tendency to evaluate ourselves in relation to others, either by looking up to those who seem better than us (upward comparison) or looking down on those who seem worse than us (downward comparison). Although some degree of social comparison is natural and inevitable, social media has amplified it to unhealthy levels. Social media platforms are built to incentivize users to showcase their accomplishments, viewpoints, and moments, but in the process, they construct a distorted and curated version of reality. We only see the highlights of other people's lives—not the struggles, failures, and challenges they face. We also tend to compare ourselves to people who are similar to us in some way, such as age, gender, or profession, which makes the comparison more salient and impactful.

Engaging in social comparison through social media can have negative consequences on our self-esteem, mood, and motivation. Research has shown that frequent exposure to social media can increase feelings of envy, dissatisfaction, loneliness, and depression. It can also lower our self-confidence, self-acceptance, and self-worth. Moreover, it can reduce our ability to appreciate what we have and enjoy our achievements. Instead of focusing on our own goals and values, we may chase external validation and approval from others. How can we cope effectively with the epidemic of social comparison? One approach is to consciously limit our time and engagement with social media, practicing mindfulness, and being selective in what we consume and share online. But there is more we can do.

Instead of comparing ourselves to others, we should be focusing on our own growth and improvement. We should celebrate our achievements—no matter how big or small—and learn from our mistakes. We should recognize our strengths and work on our weaknesses. We should appreciate and value what we have and what we can do instead of dwelling on what we lack or cannot achieve. By doing so, we boost our confidence and happiness and become more resilient and adaptable to life's challenges. Comparing ourselves to others is a natural human tendency, but healthy nor productive. It can steal our happiness and potential, leaving us feeling inferior or envious. Instead of wasting our time and energy on comparing ourselves to others, we should invest them in becoming the best version of ourselves. This way, we will not only improve our own lives but also inspire and help others along the way.

Codependency and Comparison

Codependents often fixate on people who seem to have more happiness, success, or love than they do, and may be doing so to compare themselves to others and seek validation, approval, or acceptance from them. They may also use comparison as a way of avoiding their problems or feelings of inadequacy. However, this strategy often backfires, as it only reinforces their negative self-image and makes them feel more insecure and unhappy.

You can overcome the habit of comparing yourself to others with the following tips:

1. **<u>Challenge distorted beliefs:</u>** This is recognizing and challenging distorted thoughts and beliefs making you feel inferior or unworthy.
1. **<u>Practice gratitude:</u>** Foster appreciation for what you have and recognize your strengths and achievements.
2. **<u>Focus on Your Goals:</u>** Prioritize your goals and values, directing your attention toward them rather than being preoccupied with the thoughts and actions of others.
3. **<u>Surround Yourself with Supportive Family and Friends:</u>** Especially when you participate often in social media, it can be difficult to find genuinely supportive friends and family members who have your best interests at heart. Surrounding yourself with loving and supportive friends and family is the best way to recognize all your good characteristics and stop comparing yourself to other people.

4. **Join a Support Group:** CoDA or Codependents Anonymous offers a valuable support network for codependents, providing a platform to listen to the experiences of others and share your own journey. This supportive environment can aid in your personal growth, helping you overcome codependency and break free from the cycle of comparison to others.

Embracing self-love and self-respect empowers you to let go of comparisons and embrace your unique journey. By focusing on your own path and embracing authenticity and joy, you can break free from the trap of constantly comparing yourself to others. When you do that, you also learn to prioritize your own needs and goals. The truth is that when you finally advocate for yourself and become your own hero, that's when you can finally start forming the loving and mutually respectful relationships you've wanted all along. It sounds cliche, but the key to loving others really is learning to love yourself.

Exercise #6

Ripley Fights Back

Becoming your own superhero involves two key aspects: establishing healthy boundaries and embracing your individual journey without comparing yourself to others. By setting effective boundaries and living authentically, you can empower yourself to be the hero of your own story. The following exercises are focused on helping you to do that.

Part 1

It's All About Boundaries

For this exercise, you will be using the acronym BOUND: Be clear, Own your feelings, Understand your needs, Negotiate respectfully, and Decide on consequences. Here is a rundown of what each letter in the acronym means:

1. **B stands for Be Clear :** Once again, go to your quiet place where you will not be disturbed. Reflect on each part of your life. You don't have to do this all at once; you can choose a different part of your life to focus on over the course of several days or weeks. Write down what you want and don't want in a specific situation or relationship. For example, "I want to spend time with my friends without feeling guilty" or "I don't want to lend money to my brother anymore." You should be as specific as you can be for each situation and relationship.
2. **is for Own Your Feelings**: Take a moment to recognize your emotions when your boundaries are either violated or honored. Reflect on how you feel in specific situations, such as "I experience frustration when my boss expects me to work additional hours without fair

compensation" or "I feel appreciated and content when my partner values and respects my opinions." By acknowledging your emotions, you gain insight into what is lacking and can identify your needs more clearly.

3. **U Stands for Understand Your Needs:** Once you have a clear understanding of your emotions related to your boundaries, take the time to identify the specific needs that contribute to your sense of safety, comfort, and respect. For instance, you might realize that you require privacy and personal space in order to feel at ease, or that honest communication is necessary for maintaining healthy relationships with your family. Being specific about your needs is essential as it paves the way for the next step in the process.

4. **N is for Negotiate Respectfully**: Effectively communicating your boundaries to others requires a calm and assertive approach. For instance, you can express your needs by saying, "I appreciate your invitation, but I'm unable to join you tonight. I need some personal time" or "I'm sorry, but I can't continue lending you money. It's not beneficial for our relationship." It's important to note that setting boundaries doesn't require you to be angry; it's simply about respecting yourself and encouraging others to do the same. By calmly stating your needs and

limits, you prioritize your well-being and ensure a more impactful message is conveyed.

5. **Decide on Consequences:** It is important to have a plan of action if your boundaries are violated or ignored. Consider the following examples: "If you continue to call me after 10 pm, I will block your number," or "If you fail to repay me by next week, I will take legal action." Similarly, you could say, "If you yell at me, I will leave and cease communication until you can speak to me respectfully," or "If you engage in physical harm, I will contact the authorities." In certain situations, it may be beneficial to document your boundaries and consequences in writing to ensure clarity and prevent any claims of unawareness. The specific actions and approach may vary depending on the nature of the relationship.

This exercise can help you practice setting strong boundaries and improve your self-esteem and well-being. It's you respecting yourself. Once you have identified your boundaries and needs, you can then communicate them to the people you believe are common violators. You can also communicate your boundaries to those who already respect them. Express your appreciation for their actions and let them know that their example has motivated you to assert these boundaries with others in your life who may not be respecting them. People who respect you will be happy you're taking this step.

Part 2

Living Your Unique Path

Comparing your experiences to others can lead to feelings of inadequacy, envy, and dissatisfaction with your own achievements and qualities, especially when you come across someone who appears to have a better situation than you. However, this habit is not only unhelpful but also unrealistic. Everyone has their own strengths and weaknesses, challenges and opportunities, and goals and values. No two people are exactly alike, and no one has a perfect life. Thus, comparing ourselves to others is like comparing apples to oranges; it does not make sense, and it does not serve us well.

One exercise to help you stop comparing yourself with others and appreciate your unique path in life is as follows:

1. **Notice the Good:** Sit in your quiet area and reflect honestly on your experiences thus far in life. Make a list of things you're proud of, enjoy doing, are skilled at, and grateful for.
2. **Make a List:** Write down 10 positive affirmations that remind you of your value and potential. Consider the following examples as baselines for your own affirmations:

- "I am enough"
- "I have something to offer to the world"
- "I am worthy of love and respect"

- "I can achieve my goals"
- "I have my own unique path and it is incredible"
  3. **Assess Your Limitations Honestly:** Next, list any limitations that may be preventing you from achieving your goals. Maybe you need to go to school and can't afford it right now, or perhaps you want to express yourself musically but don't know how to play an instrument.
  4. **Make Another List:** Now, make a list of 10 affirmations related to the limitations you noted. Consider the following examples when starting out your list:
- "I am so much more than any limitation."
- "Nothing can stop me from achieving my happiness because I am my happiness."

> Then, if you want to go to school but can't afford it, you might write, "I am intelligent and can express that in many ways." If you don't know how to play an instrument, you might write, "The music I *can* express is in my soul." Another good one is, "My limitations don't prevent me from experiencing joy," or "I am like water; I can move around any obstacle in my path." Limitations are only temporary obstacles; they don't really prevent us from moving along our unique path because there is always a way around them.

We can regularly review and update this list, allowing it to serve as a powerful tool to boost our confidence, motivation, and overall happiness. Through this exercise, we come to recognize and appreciate our inherent value and our ability to make positive contributions to the world, regardless of our current circumstances.

Final Thoughts on Saving Yourself

One of the most important things about being your own hero is learning to respect and love yourself. You have value and understanding that will unlock your potential. Once you can set your own boundaries and express them to others—and stop living your life as a comparison to others—then can you resolve those old, toxic relationships and move toward what can really make you happy. These are concepts we will explore in the coming chapters.

Chapter 7

Resolving Old, Toxic Relationships

Toxic relationships are commonly viewed as negative influences or individuals who have entered our lives. However, it is worth considering an alternative perspective: What if these relationships could be opportunities for growth and learning? What if we turn it around and make them lessons that enable us to tap into our unlimited potential? How would knowing that change your perception of those toxic relationships? How would it change your codependency? No one else's experience is any less valid than another's. Would knowing that change the way you interact with other people?

For a significant period, I found myself constantly comparing my experiences to those of others, passing judgment along the way. That's not uncommon; almost everyone does that. Upon realizing the toxicity of my narcissistic husband, I couldn't help but feel empathy toward him, recognizing my own toxic behavioral patterns and sensing the torturous state of his mind and underlying fragility. But that doesn't change the fact that I also knew I had to get away from him—I had to get out of that relationship. And what did that represent for me? It meant that I was finally understanding on some level that I didn't deserve that kind of treatment. That's a big insight to have, even though I clearly didn't see it that way at the time. And who sparked that insight in me? It was none other than my toxic husband.

I also realized that I was judging his experience as inferior to mine because of his toxicity. The reality is that everyone's experience is valid for their life's path. Both of our paths brought us together, and it helped me find a path toward healing. I can't say what our union did for his journey, but I can now see clearly what it did for mine. Although my codependency formed as a behavioral pattern long before I met him, he was the proverbial straw that broke the camel's back. He was what finally pushed me to the brink and made me seek the help I needed to heal. That's the valuable gift my husband brought into my life, illustrating how every person—good or bad—who enters our lives can still bring us something of value to learn from. Your task is to see beyond the haze created by your conditioned mind, allowing yourself to recognize and embrace the gift that each person brings into your life. Additionally, although they may cause you anxiety, it is often that discomfort that is the impetus for real change. If you're comfortable, it's easy to settle into your current situation rather than face the uncertainty of change. When you find yourself under immense pressure and experiencing pain, it often becomes a catalyst for taking action, and it is during these moments that true transformation and change can occur. But those old, toxic relationships often haunt us for years to come. So how do we go about resolving them?

What is the Legacy of Your Toxic Relationships?

Toxic relationships are those that cause harm to one or both partners, either physically, emotionally, mentally, or financially. They are characterized by a lack of trust, respect, communication, and support. My relationship with my mother was toxic, as was my relationship with many romantic partners as an adult. I was looking to please people who were only looking to exploit me. Each person had their own history of trauma that caused them to behave the ways they did. Challenging as it may be to acknowledge, even those who have caused us harm or behaved in toxic ways have their own unique journey to navigate and lessons to learn. Their experience is no less valid than mine, but that doesn't mean I have to endure the effects of their toxicity.

Toxic relationships can affect you in many ways, such as:

1. **Lowering your self-esteem and confidence:** During such times, it's common to question your self-worth and capabilities, experiencing feelings of guilt or shame. Your enthusiasm for hobbies, goals, and passions may wane as well.
2. **Damaging your mental and physical health:** These challenges can manifest in various ways, including increased stress, anxiety, depression, insomnia, headaches, and other physical or emotional symptoms. It's not uncommon to neglect your basic needs, such as proper nutrition, exercise, and sufficient sleep, during this time.
3. **Isolating you from your friends and family:** During this time, it's common to feel some loneliness and disconnection from your social network. You may find yourself avoiding or limiting contact with others, either due to your partner's jealousy, control, or manipulation, or because of your own fear of judgment or criticism.
4. **Impairing your performance and productivity:** The overwhelming stress from the toxic relationship may lead to difficulty concentrating, making decisions, or completing tasks at work, school, or home. Consequently, you might find yourself missing deadlines, skipping classes, or taking more sick days than usual.

5. **Preventing you from growing and learning:** You may stop pursuing new opportunities, challenges, or experiences that could enrich your life. You may also lose sight of your values, beliefs, and dreams.
6. **While toxic relationships can leave lasting scars:** it's important to remember that healing is possible. By acknowledging the lessons they bring and allowing yourself to receive their gifts, you can gradually move toward healthier and happier relationships. The journey to healing may take time, but with self-reflection, support, and self-care, you can create a brighter future for yourself. But to do so, you should understand how to interact with other people. Transactional analysis is a theory that views interactions as transactions, and it provides a framework for analyzing and understanding human behavior within these transactions.

Transactional Analysis: Where It Is Usually Depends on Where You Started

An individual's attachment style and experiences during psychosocial development play a significant role in shaping their psychological well-being and can contribute to various psychological disorders, including codependency. Furthermore, these factors can impact one's emotions, thoughts, and behaviors when engaging with others. When interacting with other people, the person who begins the interaction would give what is referred to as the "transaction stimulus," and then you would give what's known as the "transaction response." Psychoanalyst, Eric Berne, studied these transactions in the late 1950s. He based his analysis on Sigmund Freud's theories about how childhood experiences have a significant impact on our adult lives. In fact, those experiences, as we've seen, form the basis for how our personalities develop. Specifically, with regard to transaction analysis, how we were parented can affect the development of our three ego states: Parent, Adult, and Child.

What Berne's research demonstrated is that dysfunctional behavior in adulthood can be the result of self-limiting decisions made in childhood. Our past decisions were made out of a necessity for survival, as they were responses to the challenges we faced during our childhood. As children, we did our best to cope with those crises, and while these coping mechanisms were effective at the time, they may not be suitable for us as adults. These dysfunctional coping patterns become ingrained and create what Berne termed a "life script." He conceived of that as a pre-conscious life plan that affects how our lives play out. Changing the ineffective script and replacing it with mature coping mechanisms is the aim of transactional analysis psychotherapy, which requires a better understanding of the three "ego states." Each state is an entire system of thought, feeling, and behavior that forms the basis of how we interact with each other. Let's examine the three ego states a little more closely.

Child Ego State

The child ego state is activated when we respond to others based on the internal emotions that were conditioned in us during our childhood. In essence, we're reverting back to a time when we were children and felt the same way. Everyone, to some degree, reverts to this state when around their parents or primary childhood caregivers. The child state consists of two subdivisions: the adapted child and the free child.

The adapted child is the ego state that seeks to conform to the wishes of others so our actions please them. We want to be seen as good, and we want to be liked. This actually has very long evolutionary roots, since not being liked could have resulted in ostracization, which, in our ancestors, was a death sentence. Even so, the adapted child has a rebellious side. It causes us to respond with emotional reactivity, resistance, and even hostility in the face of conflict. The free child state is that side of each of us that is creative, spontaneous, playful, and pleasure-seeking. Your individual child ego state is shaped by the reinforcements and experiences you received during your childhood. They can be either positive or negative, but these childhood experiences shape your behavior in certain situations and continue to influence your interactions today.

Parent Ego State

This state also has two subdivisions: the critical/controlling parent and the nurturing parent. In both cases, we learn our parent state from our parents and other authority figures. Berne argued that it is our experiences in the first five years of our life that form the parent ego state. This state of mind is where you form judgments about how someone should or shouldn't be or what they should or shouldn't do. When you're reactive to a situation and simply act from a place of conditioned responses, you're in the parent ego state. Basically, you copy what your parents or other authority figures did rather than analyze the situation from a fresh perspective. This is also known as the "Don't run with a sharp stick, you'll put your eye out" state of conditioning. When interacting from the parent ego state, you may use an authoritative voice, and if you're in the critical parent state, you might express disapproval in harsh and sometimes aggressive ways. If you're in the nurturing parent ego state, you are looking at the situation from a protective perspective. You're trying to soothe someone, but sometimes that can be done inappropriately.

Adult Ego State

This state doesn't have any subdivisions; it is the egoic state where you interact with other people and your environment in the present moment. Essentially, you're in the here and now rather than responding from past conditioning. This is an open, more rational, and less judgmental state. Interactions will likely be more respectful and open to compromise, and you will listen more carefully to others, usually resulting in healthier social interactions.

Your ego state during any given interaction depends on several factors—one of these is how you were conditioned to act or react as a child. If you experienced childhood trauma, it can influence the ego state you find yourself in when triggered by similar circumstances, actions, or words. Often, those past traumas cause us to default subconsciously to either the parent ego state or the child ego state, which are the simplest and fastest reaction states because we don't think about them. We essentially react from a conditioned state. To bring ourselves into the adult ego state, we have to *think* about it. We have to bring ourselves into the present and think about the situation we're in before interacting.

Berne noticed that people need what he referred to as *units of interpersonal recognition* to survive and thrive. Basically, you need your props, and your strokes. People have the capacity to provide either positive or negative feedback, which are referred to as "strokes" in transactional analysis. Recognizing and changing unhealthy patterns of strokes is crucial in helping individuals address conditioned responses and develop a more adult ego state when engaging with others. The objective is to facilitate effective adult communication by encouraging both parties to engage from an adult ego state, promoting healthy and constructive interactions while fostering understanding, empathy, and mutual respect.

My background was one of a very critical mother, and because of that, my conditioned parent ego state is quite judgmental. Frequently, my response to aggressive interactions stemmed from a conditioned child ego state, leading me to react in familiar patterns. The conditioning was so strong, in fact, that bringing myself back into an adult ego state was extremely challenging. This is true of many codependents—they've been conditioned to put their own needs aside to focus on pleasing other people.

Characteristics of Unhealthy Transactions

Toxic relationships are usually characterized by unhealthy interpersonal transactions—so resolving your transactional behaviors would be key to resolving your old, toxic relationships. Unhealthy interpersonal transactions are interactions that harm the well-being of one or both parties involved. They can take various forms, such as manipulation, abuse, neglect, exploitation, or violence. Some characteristics of unhealthy interpersonal transactions include:

1. **Lack of respect:** One or both parties do not value the other's feelings, opinions, boundaries,

or rights. They may disregard, criticize, insult, or mock the other person.
2. **Lack of trust:** One or both parties do not believe in the other's honesty, integrity, or reliability. They may doubt, accuse, lie to, or betray the other person.
3. **Lack of communication:** One or both parties do not express their needs, feelings, or expectations clearly and openly. They may avoid, ignore, withhold, or distort information from the other person.
4. **Lack of reciprocity:** One or both parties do not give and take equally in the relationship. They may demand, expect, or take more than they offer, contribute, or share with the other person.
5. **Lack of support:** One or both parties do not provide emotional, practical, or financial assistance to the other when needed. They may neglect, reject, or undermine the other person's goals, interests, or well-being.

Unhealthy interpersonal transactions can have negative consequences for both parties involved. They can damage their self-esteem, mental health, physical health, and social relationships. Therefore, it is important to recognize and avoid unhealthy interpersonal transactions and seek help if needed.

Transactional Analysis and Codependency

Codependent people are those who depend excessively on others for their emotional needs, often sacrificing their own well-being and identity to do so. Codependent individuals often engage in dysfunctional transactions with others, where their ego states are incongruent or mismatched. For instance, a codependent person may assume a child role, seeking validation from a partner who adopts a parent role. Alternatively, a codependent person may take on a parent role, attempting to control or rescue a partner who behaves as a child. These transactions result in power imbalances and hinder the authentic expression of emotions and needs for both individuals involved.

Codependent people also tend to have distorted perceptions of themselves and others, which can affect their transactions. They may have low self-esteem and feel unworthy of love and respect, or they may have unrealistic expectations and demands of others. They may also deny or ignore their own feelings and needs or project them onto others. These perceptions lead to unhealthy patterns of communication and behavior, such as manipulation, guilt-tripping, blaming, passive-aggressiveness, avoidance, or withdrawal. Codependent people can benefit from transactional analysis therapy, which aims to help them identify and change their dysfunctional transactions and perceptions. Through increased self-awareness of their ego states and their impact on interpersonal interactions, individuals can acquire valuable skills in effective and assertive communication. By acknowledging and validating their own emotions and needs, they can prioritize self-care and establish internal boundaries. Furthermore, by cultivating a balanced and realistic perception of themselves and others, they can foster healthier and more fulfilling relationships.

Setting Appropriate Internal Boundaries to Improve Transactions

Setting internal boundaries is a crucial skill for anyone who wants to improve their interpersonal transactions—particularly for codependent people. Internal boundaries are the limits and expectations that we set for ourselves and others in our personal and professional relationships. They help us communicate clearly, respect our own and others' needs and preferences, and avoid unnecessary conflict and misunderstandings. Setting internal boundaries can improve interpersonal transactions in three ways: by enhancing self-awareness, fostering mutual respect, and promoting healthy collaboration.

1. **Increase Self-Awareness:** Setting internal boundaries can enhance self-awareness, which is the foundation of any successful interpersonal transaction. Self-awareness is the ability to recognize and understand one's own emotions,

thoughts, values, strengths, weaknesses, and motivations. Setting internal boundaries helps us understand our wants, needs, and limitations. It allows us to recognize triggers and challenges in different situations, promoting self-awareness and healthy interactions with others. This can help us to avoid projecting our issues onto others, take responsibility for our own actions and reactions, and express ourselves authentically and confidently.

2. **Foster Mutual Respect:** Setting internal boundaries can foster mutual respect, which is the key to any harmonious interpersonal transaction. Mutual respect involves acknowledging and valuing the inherent worth, uniqueness, and dignity of both ourselves and others. Setting internal boundaries allows us to respect ourselves by honoring our feelings, opinions, and choices, and by asserting ourselves when necessary. We can also show respect for others by listening to their perspectives, acknowledging their feelings, and honoring their boundaries. This can help us build trust, rapport, and understanding with others while avoiding conflict and resentment.

3. **Promote Healthy Collaboration:** Setting internal boundaries can promote healthy collaboration, which is the goal of any productive interpersonal transaction. Setting internal boundaries facilitates healthy

collaboration by clarifying roles and responsibilities, effective communication of expectations and feedback, and respecting diversity and creativity, enabling individuals to work together toward a common purpose or goal in a mutually beneficial manner. This can then help us achieve our objectives more efficiently, learn from each other's experiences and insights, and celebrate our achievements together. Setting internal boundaries enhances self-awareness, fosters mutual respect, and promotes healthy collaboration, resulting in more enriching personal and professional relationships.

4. We talked about setting boundaries in the previous chapter, and while the exercise in that chapter can help you set your boundaries, internal boundaries are all about you respecting yourself. Just like you wouldn't allow someone else to devalue you, you can't accept devaluation from your inner critic. If you devalue yourself, you won't even recognize the devaluation someone else uses against you as abusive. It is so—whether it comes from you or anyone else. Before you can resolve your old, toxic relationships, you must first value yourself enough to practice self-compassion, self-forgiveness, and true self-love.

Exercise #7

Resolution

Resolution involves a bit more work to heal thoroughly, so this exercise is in three parts. First, it's important to recognize the transactional nature of the toxic relationship and understand the reasons behind your feelings of trauma. Next, you can work toward implementing healthier and more positive forms of interpersonal transactions. By doing so, you can begin the healing process and address the wounds from the past. Let's start with identifying the problem.

Part 1

Identification

One way to practice using internal boundaries is to identify a situation where you felt angry, or resentful toward someone else. It could be a family member, friend, coworker, or anyone else. Write down what happened, how you felt, and what you did or said in response. Then, reflect on the following questions:

- What boundary was crossed or violated by the other person?
- How did you express your boundary to them? Was it clear and assertive or vague and passive?
- How did they react to your boundary? Did they respect, ignore, or challenge it?

- How did you feel after the interaction? Relieved, guilty, frustrated, or something else?
- What could you do differently next time to set and maintain a healthier internal boundary?

This exercise can help you become more aware of your own internal boundaries and how they affect your interpersonal transactions. It can also help you improve your skills in setting and communicating your boundaries to others respectfully and effectively.

Part 2

Implementation

Think again about the situation you identified in Part 1 of this exercise. Think about what triggered your negative emotions and what you wanted to say or do at that moment. Then, write down three possible responses that you could have given using internal boundaries. For example:

- **Situation**: Your boss asks you to work overtime on a project that is not your responsibility.
- **Trigger**: You feel overworked, unappreciated, and taken advantage of.
- **Possible responses**:
❖ "I'm sorry, but I can't work overtime on this project. It's not part of my job description and I have other priorities to attend to."
❖ "I appreciate your confidence in me, but I'm not available to work overtime on this project. It's

outside my scope of work, and I have other commitments that I need to honor."

❖ "No, thank you. I'm not interested in working overtime on this project. It's not aligned with my goals and values, and I have other plans for my time."

Try to use assertive language, and express your feelings and needs clearly—while respecting the other person's feelings and needs as well. Avoid blaming, criticizing, or judging the other person or agreeing to something that you don't want to do. Remember that you have the right to say no, and that you are responsible for your own happiness and well-being.

Part 3

Healing Old Toxic Relationships

One way to heal old, toxic relationships is to improve your interpersonal transactions. Interpersonal transactions are the exchanges of words, gestures, and emotions that happen between two or more people. They can be positive, negative, or neutral. In this exercise, you will learn how to identify and change your interpersonal transactions to make them more positive and constructive.

- **Consider the Relationship You Want to Heal:** Think of an old, toxic relationship that you want to heal. It can be with a family member, friend, colleague, or anyone else. Write down the name of the person and the reason why the relationship is toxic.

- **Recall Your Transactional Style with Them:** Recall some interpersonal transactions that you had with that person in the past. Write down at least three examples of what you said or did, and how the person reacted. Try to be as specific and honest as possible.
- **Analysis:** Analyze each interpersonal transaction that you wrote down. Use the following questions to guide you:

❖ Was the transaction positive, negative, or neutral?
❖ How did it affect your and the other person's feelings?
❖ What was the underlying message or intention behind the transaction?
❖ How could you have said or done something different to make the transaction more positive?

Write down your answers for each transaction.

1. **Practice, Practice, Practice:** Practice changing your interpersonal transactions with that person. Imagine that you have a chance to talk to them again and write down what you would say or do differently using the insights from your analysis. Try to use positive words, gestures, and emotions that show respect, and empathy.
2. **How Can It Help?:** Reflect on how changing your interpersonal transactions can help you heal the old, toxic relationship. Write down how you

feel after doing this exercise. Do you feel more hopeful, confident, or relieved? Do you think the other person would respond differently if you used these new transactions? Can you see their point of view with compassion? How would that affect your relationship?

This exercise can help you improve your interpersonal transactions and heal old, toxic relationships. By changing your words, gestures, and emotions, you can create more positive and constructive exchanges with others. This can lead to more trust and harmony in your relationships. It can also help you better understand what exactly was wrong the first time around. You can foster compassion toward both the person and their behavioral style, while also showing compassion toward yourself and your own reactions. This compassionate perspective can aid in overcoming the lingering effects of the toxic relationship, as it allows you to gain insight into what went wrong and how you would approach things differently now.

As a final note, this exercise can help with writing a letter to the person involved in the toxic relationship. Through personal growth and reflection, you can gain a deeper understanding of the motivations behind the actions of both yourself and the other person in the toxic relationship. This understanding allows you to recognize the underlying reasons for their behavior and your own reactions; it brings clarity to the dynamics of the relationship and enables you to make sense of the past.

You can offer them your forgiveness, whether or not you ever want them in your life again. You can send the letter to them or not as well; it doesn't matter. What matters is that you've expressed yourself and processed those emotions.

Final Thoughts on Resolving Old, Toxic Relationships

Healing those old, unhealthy relationships is vital for moving forward. If you don't do this work, you will dwell on them, even if only in your subconscious mind. When you resolve them, then can you truly let go of your past and move forward with your future. You're free from the prison the toxicity created in your mind. Your past becomes merely a series of events that happened to you as opposed to an integral part of your identity. Through the process of self-reflection and personal growth, you can come to the realization that you deserve better treatment and that you played a role in allowing the toxic relationship to persist. This realization empowers you to take responsibility for your own well-being and make choices that align with your self-worth and self-respect. You can fully understand the problem, see it in a compassionate light, and cultivate forgiveness for both your abusers and yourself. Whether or not they ever change, apologize, or even understand the wounds they inflicted is of no consequence. What matters is that you see it, and you've let it go. Now, you can truly seek the road to a happier life.

Chapter 8

The Road to a Happier You

Healing from codependency can be likened to receiving a "get out of jail" free card, where you experience the liberation of a prisoner who has been proven innocent. It marks the start of a transformative journey, fostering a fresh and profound connection with yourself. Furthermore, it paves the way for renewed relationships with those around you, allowing for healthier dynamics and interactions. Make no mistake; there may be some people who have grown accustomed to the old, people-pleasing version of you and might be taken aback by the changes in your behavior. Those are the people you might choose to say goodbye to as you forge a new path for yourself. But freeing yourself from the chains of codependency is just the first step in the journey. You'll find there are other wounds you'll have to heal along the way too. The wounds that created your codependency likely left other scars as well. It's crucial to dedicate time to heal those aspects of yourself. Additionally, it's important to acknowledge that even after healing, you may encounter a range of emotions, including some that might catch you by surprise. You've been living a certain way for a long time now, and it's all about to change, so how do you go forward, and what other challenges might you encounter?

What Emotions Will You Notice?

Healing from codependency involves recognizing and changing unhealthy patterns of behavior and developing a sense of self-worth, autonomy, and assertiveness. It also involves learning to prioritize your own needs and feelings and set healthy limits with others. Healing from codependency can be a challenging and rewarding process, and it can evoke a range of emotions along the way. All reactions are valid, and it's essential to be prepared for the variety of emotions you may experience.

Some emotions you might feel once you've healed your codependent patterns include:

1. **Relief:** You may feel relieved that you no longer have to carry the burden of someone else's issues or endure their abuse or manipulation. You may feel free from the stress and anxiety that plagued you in your codependent relationship. It may also be comforting to know that you can finally

focus on yourself and your own goals without feeling guilty or selfish.

2. **Joy:** Discovering new aspects of yourself, your interests, and your passions can evoke a sense of joy. Cultivating healthy relationships built on mutual respect, trust, and support can bring forth feelings of elation, and recognizing your worthiness of love and happiness and embracing the power to create a fulfilling life may fill you with delight.

3. **Anger:** Reflecting on how your codependent relationship harmed you or how the other person took advantage of you can evoke feelings of anger. Recognizing the injustice and unfairness of what you endured may also ignite anger within you. Additionally, confronting the underlying causes of your codependency, such as childhood trauma or family dysfunction, may stir up anger. It is important to remember that anger can be a healthy and empowering emotion, as long as you express it constructively and prevent it from overwhelming you.

4. **Grief:** Experiencing grief is natural as you navigate the aftermath of your codependent relationship and the person you were during that time. It is normal to mourn the loss of the relationship and the accompanying hopes and dreams you had. Letting go of the fantasy of what could have been and accepting the reality of your situation may also evoke feelings of

grief. While grief can be painful, it is an important emotion that allows you to process your loss and embark on the journey of moving forward.

5. **Pride:** Recognizing your progress and growth in your healing journey can evoke feelings of pride. You may take pride in celebrating your achievements and accomplishments, regardless of their size. Embracing your strengths, talents, and inherent value can also generate a sense of pride. It is important to channel this emotion in a positive and motivating way, avoiding the pitfalls of arrogance or complacency. Pride can serve as a reminder of your resilience and serve as a catalyst for further personal growth.

6. **Depression:** You may also feel some level of depression while orienting yourself to the possibilities in your life now. Although you're no longer carrying the burden of someone else's needs and desires, you may feel uncertain about the path your life will take now. You may wonder what your purpose is if you are no longer serving someone else. This does not mean that the healing has not been effective. It's something to expect as you define the direction your life will take now that you're finally free.

There is nothing wrong with anything you might feel, but you might not expect to experience negative emotions. Emotional fluctuations are normal during the healing process, and it's important to realize that codependency may not be the only behavioral pattern you've picked up through the years. Let's take a look at some of the other patterns you might have developed.

What Other Behavioral Patterns are Common in Codependents?

As codependency developed, it is likely that you also adopted other ingrained patterns of behavior. Here are some common ones that may be part and parcel of your codependency.

1. **Confluence:** This is when a person loses their sense of individuality and merges with others or the environment. They may avoid conflict and try to please everyone. They may also have difficulty expressing their feelings and opinions.
2. **Introjection:** This is when a person passively accepts the values and attitudes of others without questioning or evaluating them. They may internalize the expectations of others and try to live up to them. They may also have low self-esteem and lack of autonomy. Introjected beliefs can be like a ghost fluttering around in the halls of your mind, whispering certain judgmental concepts in your ear. It can affect your behavior on a subliminal level, and it is very difficult to recognize.
3. **Projection:** This is when a person denies or rejects an aspect of themselves and attributes it to someone else. They may see in others what

they do not want to see in themselves. They may also blame others for their own problems or criticize others for their own faults. When this happens, you know it's part of your shadow, and although you may have addressed other shadows, each time you encounter one, it's important to welcome that part of yourself into the light as well.

4. **Retroflection:** This is when a person turns their actions or feelings back onto themselves instead of expressing them outwardly. They may do to themselves what they want to do to others or what they want others to do to them. They may also suppress their anger or hurt and harm themselves instead. This is another very common pattern in codependents. Our entire self-value is based on what we can do for others, and we fall all over ourselves trying not to hurt them, no matter how much we might be hurting ourselves.

5. **Deflection:** This is when a person avoids direct contact or communication with themselves or others. They may distract themselves from their own feelings or issues by changing the subject, making jokes, or being vague. They may also avoid intimacy or commitment by keeping a distance from others. You might feel this for a while out of fear that you will fall back into a pattern of codependency. But distraction and avoidance is never the answer; self-respect and self-compassion is the way.

6. **Proflexion:** This is when a person anticipates future events or outcomes and reacts to them as if they were already happening. They may worry excessively about what might go wrong or what others might think of them. They may also miss out on the present by living in the future. As a codependent, I did this all the time to avoid negative feedback from others in my life. It's also a common pattern among people who want to have a plan for every possible outcome. They don't want life to surprise them, and they try to anticipate everything that might happen.
7. **Egotism:** This is when a person has an exaggerated sense of self-importance and superiority over others. They may believe they are always right and their needs and opinions are more valuable than those of others. They may also lack empathy or compassion for others and exploit them for their own benefit. Once you've freed yourself of codependence, it can be easy for the pendulum to swing too far to the other side. You may go overboard in valuing your own needs to the point of becoming egotistic.

Understanding these patterns can help you become more aware of your own behavior and make positive changes if needed or avoid pitfalls after you've healed. It's important to address any other negative patterns you might have developed alongside your codependency as well. Unfortunately, for complicated conditions like this, there are often a number of other habits we've fallen into; now that you've developed a heightened sense of self-awareness, you're much better equipped to recognize unproductive behavioral strategies and make positive changes. By doing so, you set yourself up for success in discovering your life's purpose and making strides toward accomplishing your goals. But how do you go about that?

How Do You Identify Your Life's Purpose?

Finding your life's purpose can be a challenging albeit rewarding journey. It can help you feel more fulfilled, motivated, and aligned with your values. But how do you discover what your purpose is? Here are some steps you can take to explore your passions, talents, and goals.

1. **Reflect on your strengths and interests**: What are you good at? What do you enjoy doing? What makes you feel alive and energized? These can serve as indicators or hints toward your life's purpose. You might also ask yourself what you love to do, even if you're not being paid to do it. Can you turn that into something that can fulfill your desires in life? You'll want to think about this creatively. For instance, if you have a passion for painting but recognize the challenges of making a sustainable income as an artist, you may need to explore alternative career paths that can provide financial stability for yourself and your dependents. Is there another way you could

work as an artist without relying solely on selling your paintings? You could teach art classes or work in an arts and crafts store. There isn't just one way to create a life that fulfills your purpose.

2. **Experiment with different activities and experiences:** Try new things that spark your curiosity or challenge you to grow. You might find something that resonates with you or reveals a hidden potential. Perhaps you love nature and being out in the natural world. Join a hiking club and see if being out regularly in nature is something that continues to make you feel fulfilled. Then you can explore ways you might turn that into a career. You might also volunteer doing something that interests you to see if it's a lasting interest or just a passing fad.

3. **Seek feedback and guidance:** Talk to people who know you well or who have similar interests. Ask them what they think your purpose is or how they found theirs—you might get some valuable insights or inspiration from doing so. Sometimes, the people we are closest to see things in us that we don't realize are there. Sometimes, we are too close to ourselves to evaluate our strengths and weaknesses objectively or recognize our true talents and abilities.

4. **Align your purpose with your values and vision:** Think about what matters most to you and what kind of impact you want to have in the

world. How does your purpose fit with these aspirations? How can you use your purpose to serve others and make a difference? You might even write your own obituary. It may sound morbid at first, but what is it you want it to say? In contemplating our lives, our hope is that others will acknowledge the significance of our actions, the positive transformations we've facilitated, and the meaningful bonds we've forged. We aspire to be remembered for making a difference, inspiring joy, and leaving a lasting legacy of love and positivity. This can help you determine your purpose in life.

Once you believe you've identified your purpose in life, you'll likely need to identify a set of goals to achieve that potential fully. That's the next step in creating your happiest life.

How Do You Set Appropriate Goals?

Once you've freed yourself from that unwanted responsibility of other people's happiness, it's time to focus on your own. This means identifying and setting goals. Goals help us to clarify our vision, focus our efforts, and measure our progress. However, not all goals are created equal. Some goals may be too vague, unrealistic, or irrelevant to our true needs and aspirations. How can we identify and set goals that are reasonable and achievable? Here are some tips to guide you.

Use the SMART Criteria

SMART stands for Specific, Measurable, Achievable, Relevant, and Time-bound. A SMART goal is clear, concrete, realistic, aligned with your values and priorities, and has a deadline. For example, instead of saying "I want to lose weight," a SMART goal would be "I want to lose 10 pounds in three months by following a healthy diet and exercising three times a week." Now that you're focusing on what you want to achieve in life, you can list what you'll need to do to achieve that goal. For instance, if you want to lose that 10 pounds, you'll first need to determine what kind of diet plan you'll follow, get the food in the house, eliminate other types of food from the house, determine an exercise routine, get a scale, and set a start date. These then become milestones you'll need to meet on the journey toward your goal. Similarly, if you decide you want to pursue a new career, you might need to get the appropriate education, and to do that, you should determine which school to go to, apply to that school, and secure the funding to pay for it.

The path to achieving your goal may appear overwhelming at times, but by breaking it down into smaller, attainable milestones, you can make it much more manageable. You can also think of it this way—the time is going to pass whether you're working toward your goal or not, so you might as well be working toward something that will ultimately bring you fulfillment and make you happy.

Break It Down

To overcome the overwhelming feeling of a daunting goal, we can break it down into smaller, more manageable steps that are more attainable and within reach. As in the example above, you would make a list of the steps you'll need to take to achieve your goal. Then, you can establish a timeline for accomplishing each step, ensuring that you progress steadily toward your goal within a structured timeframe.

When I made the decision to pursue a degree in psychology, there were several steps I needed to take. First, I had to research and choose the schools I wanted to apply to. Then, I completed the application process for each school, ensuring that I met all the requirements. Next, I focused on securing the necessary funding to cover the expenses associated with my education. Additionally, I had to plan and organize the logistics of relocating to the area where the school was located, including finding suitable housing. Alongside these practical considerations, I also had to plan my course schedule carefully and acquire the necessary materials for each class. These were just some of the many steps involved in pursuing my goal of obtaining a degree in psychology. That's a lot, but you can set a timetable for each part. It works really well, for example, to break down the steps in the process into daily, weekly, monthly, and yearly milestones. To effectively manage your goals and stay organized, it's helpful to establish a regular routine for reviewing and planning. On a daily basis, take time to review and outline the tasks and objectives you aim to accomplish for that day. Each week, dedicate a day to assess your progress, set targets, and plan for the upcoming week. Similarly, on a monthly basis, take the opportunity to plan for the next while reflecting on your achievements from the previous. Lastly, on an annual basis, set overarching goals for the upcoming year and reflect on your accomplishments and growth from the past year. By implementing these regular review and planning sessions, you can stay focused, motivated, and on track toward achieving your goals. Treat it like you're the CEO of your business, which is working toward achieving your happiest life. Use a daily, weekly, and monthly planner to set your milestones and schedule meetings to review your progress and plan for what comes next. You're much more likely to stick to this process if you formalize it. Making plans like this also gives you a material list that you can check off each time you complete a milestone. This is a very satisfying feeling.

Adapt Milestones and Goals as Necessary

Our goals are not set in stone. They can change over time as we learn new information, face new challenges, or discover new opportunities. Therefore, it is important to review and adjust your goals regularly to make sure they are still relevant and realistic. You can use feedback from others, self-reflection, or performance indicators to evaluate your progress and identify areas that need improvement. This is the benefit of the planner. As you conduct meetings with yourself, you can review your milestones and goals to see if you are still excited to complete them. If something has changed, you can make the necessary adjustments. For example, while pursuing my degree in psychology, I initially had the goal of obtaining a general psychology degree. However, as I progressed in my education and explored various areas within psychology, my interests evolved, leading me to adjust my focus and explore different specializations and career paths. This flexibility allowed me to align my studies and future goals with my evolving passions and interests in the field of psychology. Even minor goals like losing that 10 pounds in three months might change later. You might discover weightlifting as a passion, but instead of just losing weight, your focus may shift toward becoming more muscular and toned. Muscle weighs more than fat, so while you may not see a significant decrease in overall weight as originally anticipated, the weight you retain or even gain is attributed to the healthier composition of muscle, resulting in a more aesthetically pleasing and toned physique.

Celebrate!

Celebrate your achievements and learn from your failures. Setting and achieving goals is not a linear process; there will be ups and downs along the way, and it is important to celebrate your achievements and reward yourself for your hard work. When you achieve a milestone along the way, determine some kind of reward you will give yourself. It can be as simple as treating yourself to a meal at your favorite restaurant or taking a well-deserved day off to relax and unwind. Whatever form it takes, make sure to allocate time to reward yourself for each milestone achieved. This is also a good time to express your gratitude for what you have accomplished and have now; doing so can boost your motivation and confidence. At the same time, it is also important to learn from your failures and mistakes. This will help you overcome obstacles and grow from your experiences. When you make a mistake or experience a failure, reflect on what happened that didn't work, and write down what you could have done better to prevent that from happening. This way, you can avoid making the same mistakes over and over again.

By following these tips, you can start moving forward toward your best life. It really doesn't matter how long it takes to reach your overall goal; what matters is that you're focusing on your goals, dreams, and happiness. By taking intentional action and making conscious choices, you have the power to shape your life according to your desires. This proactive approach is also essential in building healthy, supportive, and mutually respectful relationships with others.

Exercise #8

Your Happy Life

As the CEO of Happier You, Inc., your job is to lay out the company's (your) goals that are in line with your values and set an agenda for achieving those goals. This two-part exercise will help you do just that. We'll start with identifying the goals, and then move on to the agenda.

Part 1

Identify Your Goals

One of the most important steps in personal development is identifying the goals that are in line with your life purpose. This exercise will help you to clarify what you want to achieve and why.

1. **Write down your life purpose statement:** This is a sentence that summarizes what you believe is the meaning of your existence and what you want to contribute to the world.

2. **Brainstorm a list of possible goals that are related to your life purpose:** These can be short-term or long-term, personal or professional, specific or general.
3. **Evaluate each goal using the SMART criteria:** Specific, Measurable, Achievable, Relevant, and Time-bound. Make sure each goal is clear, realistic, and aligned with your life purpose.
4. **Prioritize your goals based on their importance and urgency:** You can use a matrix to rank them according to four categories: Important and Urgent, Important but Not Urgent, Not Important but Urgent, and Not Important and Not Urgent.
5. **Create a timeline:** Choose one or two goals from each category that you want to focus on for the next week, month, quarter, or year. Write down an action plan for each goal, detailing the steps you need to take, the resources you need, and any deadlines.
6. **Review your goals and action plans regularly:** Track your progress and celebrate your achievements. Adjust your goals and plans as needed based on your feedback and changing circumstances.

Part 2

Create Your Agenda

The next step after creating your goals and laying out a timeline is to organize your agenda. You want to have daily time for reflection and planning, a weekly meeting for organizing and reviewing, a monthly meeting for laying out the next month's agenda and assessing your progress, and a yearly meeting to chart your progress and plan for the next year's agenda. You're much more likely to be successful in following an agenda if you stay consistent in your time. For each of the prompts below, lay out a plan for your company's meetings.

1. Every day at _____ AM/PM, I will take _____ minutes to practice mindfulness around the day's goals, review the previous day's progress, and plan for the current day.
2. On _____ (Choose a day of the week), I will take _____ (hour/hours) at _____ AM/PM to plan for the upcoming week and review the progress made in the previous week.
3. On _____ (DATE), I will meet for _____ (length of time) to review the previous month's progress and plan the next month's agenda.
4. On _____ (DATE), I will meet for _____ (length of time) to review the

previous year's accomplishments and set the agenda for the upcoming year.

Once you've laid out your agenda, you can now put the dates and times into your calendar and set reminders as appropriate. It's also important to build self-care time into your agenda, and you might consider planning for that in a similar manner.

Final Thoughts on Your Road to Happiness

As a recovering codependent, embarking on the journey of discovering your life's purpose and setting meaningful goals is a significant stride away from the negative behavioral patterns associated with codependency. It signifies your commitment to personal growth and cultivating a healthier and more fulfilling life. You're now working toward your own happiness and success, and that's a huge change for the better. As you continue to grow in confidence and satisfaction, you'll be even more motivated to keep going, and you'll also have much more to be grateful for when you celebrate your achievements. To help fulfill your goals, we'll talk in the next chapter about implementing new habits as you move forward with your new life.

Chapter 9

New Habits, New Life

Now that you have liberated yourself from codependency and defined the goals you wish to pursue in your life, there are numerous new, healthier habits and strategies that you can adopt as you move forward. These practices will support your personal growth and contribute to a more fulfilling and balanced life. For me, this involved prioritizing my self-care, regardless of everything else going on in my life. I suspect that's true for many codependents. I had a bad habit of not attending to my own needs if any other part of my life stressed me out. The problem with that is that there's always something stressful happening at any given time in your life. I used to believe that I would find the time to prioritize self-care when I had less stress in my life, but the truth is, I was constantly feeling overwhelmed and stressed. What's more, the self-care activities I needed to prioritize were those that would help to alleviate my stress.

The truth is that life's a challenge, and there will always be something that's stressing you out, even if it's good stress. So you need to make self-care a habit that you prioritize as much as you would eating regularly or brushing your teeth. You also need to make your new coping mechanisms, like learning to listen to intuition or your body, into habits as well. As a codependent, your brain adopted a habit of constantly seeking out problems that other people were experiencing, so you would rush to help them. That was something that helped you survive as a child, but now it's time to take care of yourself. Now, you need to train your brain to use positive self-talk, self-trust, and self-care as mechanisms for reacting to stress, rather than negative, self-punishing ones. So how do you change your habits?

Take Off Your Mask

One of the most influential concepts in psychology is the idea of the persona, developed by Carl Jung. The persona is a mask or role that we present to the world, especially in social situations. It is not our true self, but rather, a compromise between our inner nature and the expectations of society. The persona helps us fit in, conform, and avoid conflict. However, Jung also warned that the persona can become a problem if we identify too much with it and lose touch with our authentic self. [Jung defined the persona](#) as "a kind of mask, designed on the one hand to make a definite impression upon others, and on the other to conceal the true nature of the individual." He proposed that each individual possesses a unique psychological makeup, referred to as the individuum. However, this individuum often clashes with societal norms and values, referred to as the collective. Thus, we create a persona to bridge the gap between our individuality and our social roles. The persona is not a fixed or static entity, but instead a flexible and adaptable one. We can change our persona depending on the situation and the audience. For example, we may act differently at work, at home, or with friends.

The persona is not necessarily a bad thing. In fact, Jung considered it as a necessary and useful function of the psyche. It allows us to communicate and cooperate with others, express ourselves in appropriate ways, and protect ourselves from criticism or rejection. It also helps us achieve our goals and aspirations. Without a persona, we would be exposed and vulnerable, unable to cope with the demands and challenges of life. However, Jung also cautioned that the persona can become a source of psychological problems if we over-identify with it and neglect our true self. He called this phenomenon "inflation of the persona." When this happens, we lose touch with our inner reality and become alienated from ourselves. We may also become rigid and inflexible in our behavior, unable to adapt to changing circumstances or new experiences. We may also develop a false sense of superiority or inferiority, depending on how we compare our persona with others. Moreover, we may suffer from inner conflict and dissatisfaction as we repress or deny aspects of ourselves that do not fit with our persona.

Jung suggested that one way to overcome the inflation of the persona is to take off the masks we put on to cope with life. He advocated for a process called individuation, which involves self-exploration and self-realization. Individuation entails becoming aware of our authentic self and integrating it with our conscious personality. It also involves acknowledging and embracing the aspects of ourselves that we have rejected or disregarded, known as the shadow. By doing so, we can achieve a balance between our inner and outer worlds and our individuum vs the overall collective. Jung's theory of the persona offers valuable insight into how we present ourselves to others and how we can relate to ourselves. You've already done much of the work proposed by Jung as part of taking off your mask. Now, you just need to learn to trust your true self. It resides inside of you, and it is always guiding you toward what is ultimately best for you. As codependents, learning to listen to our intuition is very difficult; we have developed a habit of relying on other people's suggestions as well as their judgments, but now we are on our own. That's a good thing, but listening to yourself and trusting your intuition is still a vital part of that process.

How Can You Learn to Trust Yourself?

Trust is a vital component of any healthy relationship, including the one you have with yourself. Learning to trust yourself can help you overcome self-doubt, fear, and anxiety. It can also boost your confidence, creativity, and happiness. But how can you learn to trust yourself? Here are some tips:

1. **Listen to your intuition:** Your intuition is your inner voice that guides you. It is based on your experiences, values, and feelings. When you listen to your intuition, you are trusting yourself to make good decisions and follow your own path.
2. **Accept your mistakes:** No one is perfect and everyone makes mistakes, so Instead of beating yourself up for your errors, accept them as opportunities to learn and grow. When you accept your mistakes, you are trusting yourself to handle challenges and overcome setbacks.
3. **Celebrate your achievements:** You have accomplished many things in your life, both big and small. Recognize and appreciate your achievements and acknowledge your strengths and talents. When you celebrate your achievements, you are trusting yourself to pursue your goals and dreams.
4. **Seek feedback:** Feedback from others can help you improve your skills, gain new perspectives, and discover new opportunities. Seek feedback from people who support you and want you to succeed. When you seek feedback, you are trusting yourself to be open-minded and adaptable.

5. **Be kind to yourself:** Self-compassion is the practice of treating yourself with kindness, understanding, and forgiveness. It means being supportive of yourself, especially when you are struggling or suffering. When you are kind to yourself, you are trusting yourself to cope with difficulties and heal from pain.

Learning to trust yourself is a process that takes time and effort. But it is worth it because it can transform your life for the better. By following these tips, you can build a strong and positive relationship with yourself.

Why Expressing Gratitude Can Help

Gratitude is a powerful emotion that can improve your well-being, happiness, and success, and it's a powerful way to express trust for yourself and your intuition. First, expressing gratitude can help you appreciate your achievements and recognize your strengths. When you acknowledge how far you have come and how much you have learned, you boost your self-esteem and confidence, and you learn to trust yourself more. You also avoid taking things for granted and becoming complacent. Instead, you feel motivated to keep growing and pursuing your goals. Second, expressing gratitude can enhance your relationships and social support. When you thank others for their help and support, you show them that you value and respect them. You also foster a positive and cooperative atmosphere that encourages mutual trust and understanding. By expressing gratitude, you strengthen your bonds with your family, friends, colleagues, and mentors. Third, expressing gratitude can reduce your stress and increase your resilience. When you focus on the positive aspects of your life and what you have accomplished, you reduce those negative and overwhelming emotions. Additionally, cultivating a more optimistic and hopeful outlook can aid in coping with challenges and setbacks. By expressing gratitude, you can improve your mental and emotional health, ultimately helping you appreciate your achievements, enhance your relationships, and reduce your stress.

Gratitude is feeling appreciation and thankfulness for the benefits and blessings we receive in life. It is a powerful and positive emotion that can enhance our well-being, happiness, and relationships. However, gratitude is not something that comes naturally to everyone; some people may struggle to feel or express gratitude, especially in difficult or stressful situations. How can we practice expressing gratitude more often and more sincerely? Here are some tips and strategies to help you cultivate a habit of gratitude.

1. **<u>Keep a gratitude journal:</u>** A gratitude journal is a simple and effective way to record and reflect on the things you are grateful for every day. You can use a notebook, smartphone app, or any other tool that works for you. The key is to write down at least three things you are grateful for each day, preferably in the morning or before going to bed. Try to be specific and detailed and

avoid repeating the same things every day. For example, instead of writing, "I am grateful for my family," you could write, "I am grateful for the hug my daughter gave me this morning" or "I am grateful for the funny joke my brother told me yesterday." Practicing gratitude through writing can help shift your focus toward the positive aspects of life and serve as a reminder of the sources of joy and meaning in your life.

2. **<u>Share gratitude to others:</u>** Sometimes it helps to express that gratitude openly with those around you. You can do this by saying thank you, writing a note, sending a message, giving a compliment, or doing a favor. Expressing gratitude to others can strengthen your relationships, boost your self-esteem, and make others feel valued and appreciated. It can also create a positive feedback loop, where the more you express gratitude, the more you receive it from others. Try to express gratitude to at least one person every day and be genuine and specific in your appreciation. For instance, instead of saying, "Thank you for your help," you could say, "Thank you for taking the time to explain this concept to me" or "Thank you for being such a supportive and caring friend."

3. **<u>Practice gratitude meditation:</u>** Gratitude meditation is a form of mindfulness meditation that involves focusing on the things you are grateful for in the present moment. You can

practice gratitude meditation by sitting comfortably, closing your eyes, and taking a few deep breaths. Then, bring to mind something or someone you are grateful for and feel that gratitude in your body and mind. You can also repeat a mantra or affirmation, such as "I am grateful for…" or "Thank you for…" You can practice gratitude meditation for as long as you like and switch to different objects of gratitude as you wish. Gratitude meditation can help you cultivate a sense of abundance and contentment in your life while reducing stress and negative emotions.

4. **<u>Use gratitude prompts:</u>** Gratitude prompts are questions or statements that stimulate your thinking and help you generate ideas for things you are grateful for. They can be useful when you feel stuck or uninspired in your gratitude practice or when you want to explore new aspects of gratitude and expand your appreciation. You can find gratitude prompts online, in books, or create your own. Some examples of gratitude prompts include:

- What made you smile today?
- What did you learn today?
- What are you looking forward to?
- What have you overcome or achieved recently?
- What do you enjoy doing?
- What do you love about yourself?
- What are you proud of?

- ❖ What makes your life easier or more comfortable?
- ❖ What inspires you?
- ❖ What are you passionate about?

Using gratitude prompts can help you expand your perspective and discover new things to be grateful for.

5. **<u>Make gratitude a part of your routine.</u>** The best way to practice expressing gratitude is to make it a part of your daily life. You can do this by setting reminders, creating rituals, or integrating gratitude into your existing habits. For example, you can:

- ❖ Start or end your day with a gratitude journal entry.
- ❖ Say thank you to someone every time you interact with them.
- ❖ Meditate on gratitude every morning or evening.
- ❖ Write a thank-you note every week.
- ❖ Compliment someone every day.
- ❖ Do a random act of kindness every day.
- ❖ Think of three things you are grateful for every time you eat a meal.
- ❖ Review your gratitude journal entries every month.

Making gratitude a part of your routine can help you develop a consistent and sustainable practice of expressing gratitude. Expressing gratitude is not only a polite and courteous gesture (including to yourself) but also a powerful and beneficial practice that can improve your well-being, happiness, and relationships. Most important of all is that it's a powerful way to acknowledge that you trust yourself to recognize your own strengths and weaknesses, seek feedback from others, and use that feedback to improve your life. It's as much about respecting and honoring yourself as it is about thanking other people for helping you.

Healthy Habits to Support the New You

Habits are patterns of behavior that we repeat automatically and often unconsciously. Habit stacking is a technique that can help you implement new, healthy habits into your daily routine. These would include your self-care habits like regular exercise and meditation. Habits can help us save time and energy, but they can also be hard to change or break. According to the habit loop model, habits consist of three components: a cue, a routine, and a reward. A cue is a trigger that initiates a habit, such as a time of day, location, or emotion. A routine is an action that we perform in response to the cue, like brushing our teeth, checking our phone, or eating a snack. A reward is an outcome that we get from the routine, such as a feeling of freshness, satisfaction, or pleasure. The habit loop model suggests that habits are formed through a process of reinforcement and repetition. When we experience a positive reward from a routine, we associate it with the cue and strengthen the habit. The more we repeat the habit loop, the more ingrained it becomes in our brain and behavior. However, habits are not fixed and immutable; they can be modified or replaced by introducing new cues, routines, or rewards. One very effective technique for doing this is habit stacking.

Habit stacking involves linking a new habit to an existing one so that you can trigger the new behavior automatically. For example, if you want to start meditating every morning, you can stack it on top of your existing habit of brushing your teeth. This way, every time you finish brushing your teeth, you can immediately start meditating for a few minutes. Habit stacking has several benefits for creating and maintaining healthy habits. First, it reduces the need for willpower and motivation, since you are using an existing cue to trigger the new habit. Second, it helps you integrate the new habit into your lifestyle rather than adding it as an extra task. Third, it creates a positive feedback loop, as it allows you to feel good about accomplishing both the old and the new habit.

To implement habit stacking effectively, you need to follow some steps. Here are some tips on how to do it:

1. **Identify the new habit you want to create:** Make sure it is specific, measurable, achievable, relevant, and time-bound (SMART). For example, instead of saying, "I want to exercise more," say "I want to do 10 pushups every morning."
2. **Identify the existing habit that you can link the new habit to:** Choose a habit that is stable, consistent, and relevant to the new habit. For example, if you want to do pushups every

morning, you can link it to your habit of getting out of bed, drinking a glass of water, brushing your teeth.

3. **Design a clear and simple plan for how to stack the habits:** Use the formula: "After/before I [existing habit], I will [new habit] in/at the [time of day]." For example, "After I drink a glass of water in the morning, I will do 10 pushups."

4. **Write down your plan and put it somewhere visible:** Your mirror is a good place to put it since you look there everyday. This will help you remember your intention and reinforce your commitment. You can also use reminders or alarms on your phone or computer to prompt you to commit to the new habit.

5. **Start small and gradually increase the difficulty or duration of the new habit:** Don't try to do too much at once, as this can overwhelm you and make you give up. Instead, start with a small and easy version of the new habit and gradually make it harder or longer as you get used to it. For example, start with five pushups and increase by one every week until you reach ten.

6. **Track your progress and reward yourself for your achievements:** Use a calendar, journal, or app to record when you do the new habit and how it makes you feel. Celebrate your successes and reward yourself with something that brings

you joy and aligns with your goals. For instance, you can treat yourself to a nutritious snack or indulge in watching an episode of your favorite show after completing your pushups.

7. **Review and adjust your plan as needed.** Sometimes, things may not go as planned, and you may encounter challenges or obstacles that hinder your ability to maintain the new habit. Don't get discouraged or give up. Instead, review your plan and see what you can change or improve to make it easier or more enjoyable for you. For instance, if you find it hard to do pushups in the morning, you can try doing them at another time that suits you better, like perhaps at night.

Habit stacking is a powerful tool that can help you create and sustain new, healthy habits in your life. By following these steps, you can make positive changes in your behavior and well-being without relying on willpower or motivation alone. You will also cut down significantly on the amount of time you need to integrate the habit into your routine.

Exercise #9

The Path to a New You

The exercises in this chapter are designed to help you learn to trust yourself and your intuition more. As in previous chapters, there are two parts, which are geared toward helping you trust your intuition and build new habits.

Part 1

Trusting Your Intuition

One way to learn to trust your intuition is to listen to your inner voice and act on it. Here is an exercise you can try:

- Go to your quiet place where you can relax and focus.
- Close your eyes and take a few deep breaths, expanding your belly and chest.
- Think of a question or situation that you need guidance on.
- Ask your intuition for an answer or direction. You can do this silently or out loud.
- Pay attention to any feelings, images, words, or sensations that come to you. Don't judge or analyze them—just observe them.
- Write down what you received from your intuition. It may be clear or vague, but trust that it has meaning for you.
- Decide how you will act on your intuition. You can follow it completely, partially, or not at all, but be aware of the consequences of each choice.
- After you have acted on your intuition, pay attention to the results and record them in your

journal. How well did it work out for you? Are you happy you followed your intuition?
- Repeat this exercise regularly and notice how your intuition becomes stronger and more reliable over time.

Using this exercise repeatedly will help you trust your intuition more and more as you see the results of following your gut.

Part 2

Make It a Habit

Habit stacking is a technique that, as we've discussed, helps you form new habits by linking them to existing ones. For example, if you want to start meditating every morning, you can stack it on top of your current habit of brushing your teeth. Here is an exercise to practice habit stacking:

1. Identify a new habit you want to incorporate into your routine.: It should be something simple and specific, such as drinking a glass of water, reading a page of a book, or stretching for five minutes. You might even use the intuition exercise in Part 1 as the habit you want to incorporate daily.
2. Choose an existing habit that you already do every day without fail, such as waking up, having breakfast, or taking a shower. This will be your anchor habit.

3. Write down a sentence that describes how you will stack your new habit on top of your anchor habit. Use the formula: "After I [anchor habit], I will [new habit]." For example, "After I brush my teeth, I will meditate for 10 minutes," or "After I brush my teeth, I will practice the intuition exercise for 10 minutes."
4. Repeat this sentence to yourself every time you do your anchor habit, then follow through with your new habit. Do this for at least 21 days—this is the average time it takes to form a new habit.
5. Celebrate your success and enjoy the benefits of your new habit. Once the habit is well-established, you can also build upon it. For example, you can extend the time you practice them. Perhaps you go from 10 minutes of meditating to 15, or you gradually increase the reps of a new exercise you do each day.

You can use habit stacking to integrate as many new habits as you need, but you should focus on one at a time. Once one new habit is integrated, then can you move on to the next.

Final Thoughts on Your New Life

Taking off your mask, integrating new, healthier habits into your routine, learning to express gratitude, and building trust in your intuition are all part of developing your new life. As codependents, we've spent our lives trying to please other people, and it can take time to really settle into a habit of prioritizing our own needs. It can be tempting to fall back into the habit of people-pleasing, but once you've become aware of this pattern within yourself, it becomes difficult to ignore when you catch yourself doing it again. It's important to remember that prioritizing your own needs is not a selfish act—it's a necessary act. You can't form healthy relationships with other people until you have a healthy relationship with yourself. That's what freeing yourself from codependency means; you're ready to build that healthy relationship with you. This is one of the most important things you will ever do. That's why, in the next and final chapter, I'll share some thoughts on how you can maintain your budding relationship with you. You'll learn all about keeping it real.

Chapter 10

Keeping It Real

Before I go any further, I want to congratulate you on finding the courage to complete the exercises in this book and seek a new way of living. It's scary to step away from established patterns, even if they no longer serve us. After all, they say, "The devil you know is better than the one you don't." Once we fall into patterns of behavior, it takes strength and courage to break those habits and live differently. You've chosen to do just that, and you should understand just how brave that is and how much strength it took to change your life. But changing your life is exactly what you are doing, so go you!!! I applaud you and feel honored that you have included me in this remarkable accomplishment. I am so proud of you and happy I get to travel with you on this healing journey.

It's a Journey—Not a Destination

You've come a long way indeed, and you need to celebrate that fact, but it is a journey, not a destination. Living with intention and emotional maturity requires ongoing vigilance and self-care as old patterns fade away and new ones emerge. It is crucial to nurture and protect our newfound healthier mindset. Embarking on the journey to heal from codependent patterns is just the beginning of a lifelong pursuit of happiness and fulfillment. It entails prioritizing your own needs and taking the necessary actions to create a satisfying life. The following are a few things to remember on your journey.

Our Partners are Mirrors

Who you choose to be close to says a lot about your relationship with yourself. Choose wisely so you take care of your needs. Ask yourself, what's in this relationship for me? This may sound cynical, but what will this person give you? I don't mean money, I mean will they respect you and grow with you? Or will you leave them behind as they stay stuck in unhealthy patterns? What do they teach you? What do they bring to your new life and mindset? If it isn't positive, maybe they bring you another lesson or gift.

I firmly believe that we attract the right person into our lives at the right time. Each person who comes to you brings a lesson, a gift, but you have to be open to receiving it. Sometimes the gift is difficult to accept, like your codependency, but those who brought the conditions that were right for codependency to develop in you taught you a valuable lesson about loving yourself. They showed you the importance of prioritizing your needs, and now you're on a happier, healthier path for your own future. As you prioritize your own needs and focus on personal growth, you become better equipped to discern the gifts that different partners and important people bring into your life. With this newfound clarity, you can make choices that align with your values and accept the gifts that contribute to your positive growth and development. You know that you don't have to be stuck anymore. You know that you have value and that you deserve love—the *real* kind of love. That is the kind that is giving and supportive, promotes personal growth, and values you for everything you are. With that knowledge, you can finally fly!

Strengthen Your Emotional Maturity

Emotional maturity is the ability to manage one's emotions healthily and constructively. It involves being aware of one's feelings, thoughts, and needs and expressing them appropriately and respectfully. We have worked in many ways on emotional maturity throughout this book. You now have the skills to increase your self-awareness, identify your needs, and express your desires, but that's not all that emotional maturity involves. Emotional maturity also means being able to empathize with others, cope with stress and challenges, and regulate one's impulses and behaviors. You have these skills as well. Some of them you've had all along, whereas others you've learned through the process of healing. You have new coping strategies now, which will help you to regulate your impulses and behaviors appropriately. The most important thing to know about emotional maturity, however, is that it is not something you're born with; rather, it is something that you develop over time through learning and experience. Throughout this book, you've increased your emotional maturity. Here are some things you've learned:

- How to cultivate a realistic and positive self-image.
- How to set healthy boundaries and respect those of others.
- How to communicate clearly and assertively without being overly aggressive or passive.
- How to handle conflicts and disagreements calmly and respectfully.
- How to show gratitude and appreciation for what you have.
- How to express your emotions appropriately and within context.
- How to manage your stress and emotions without resorting to unhealthy coping mechanisms.

- How to seek help and support when needed.

It's important to recognize that emotional maturity is not a static state but an ongoing process that requires continuous effort and growth. It is a multifaceted concept that can vary based on different circumstances and individuals. Therefore, it is important to be mindful of your emotional maturity level and strive to enhance it throughout different aspects of life. Check in with yourself regularly and practice those vital self-care habits to grow your emotional maturity.

Take Responsibility

Finally, the journey you're on requires that you take responsibility for your life. Here's the thing about giving up your codependency habit—it's all up to you now. Now you know that your happiness, self-love, and life are all in your hands. No one else can give you these things; you have to take responsibility for making your life what you want it to be. But that's nothing to worry about. You already know you have the courage to do just that; after all, you picked up this book and ventured on this journey with me. That is an act of courage in and of itself. By embarking on this journey, you've already shown that you are ready for this responsibility. You now have the skills you need to continue growing the strong relationship you've established with yourself. I have no doubt you'll do whatever you decide you need to do going forward. That may mean many things, but from now on, it will always mean that you can take care of yourself with all the love you deserve.

You've Got This

When I first became aware of the depth of my codependency and recognized the need to address it, I was filled with fear and pain. It took that level of pain to make me take a long, hard look at myself and how my trauma had affected me. I knew something was wrong, but I didn't really know what it was. When I saw the reality, I wasn't entirely sure I could change that pattern. As I embarked on my journey of healing, however, my confidence grew daily, and I realized that I could do it. The doubts I had were little more than introjected beliefs haunting the recesses of my mind. I have finally banished those old ghosts, but I continue to work on my personal growth even today. Now, I take pride in guiding others through the darkest corners of their minds toward the light of self-love and self-worth, as I have found in my own life. But even more than that, I'm most happy that I've learned to value myself and insist on getting my needs met. I am truly like that heroic character Ripley, holding my inner child in my arms and conquering any beasts that dare to threaten our inner peace. And so are you!

If I can do this, so can you. What one person can do, so can another. You have the skills, you have a new mindset, and you have a path to follow. Take care of yourself in whatever way that is right for you. Seek out therapy if that's what you feel you need, meditate daily if that speaks to you, continue writing in your journal, take the time to get in touch with your emotions, and most of all, love yourself. Be your own hero because in the end, the one person whom you can be sure you will wake up with every morning for the rest of your life is *you*. So be kind, good, and in love with yourself, and you will find the internal peace that you seek. I know you can do it, and I want to hear all about your success story. Please feel free to contact me at Facebook www.facebook.com/elena.miro.psy and tell me about your heroic journey. Your feedback is so valuable to me, and it only takes one minute of your time to leave a review of this book. I know you're busy, but I love hearing from the people I reach—all the heroes on the same journey I'm on. I believe we are in this life to grow love, and by learning to love yourself, you're contributing to the wellness our world so desperately needs in the modern day. You're helping create a better, more compassionate place for all of us to live. As it turns out, you're not just your own hero; you're a hero for all of us, and to that, I say BRAVO!

References Cited

Co-Dependents Anonymous International. (2022, August 19). CoDA.org. CoDA.org. https://coda.org/.

Diamond, S. A. (2008, June 7). Essential Secrets of Psychotherapy: The Inner Child: Has your adult self spent time with your inner child today? Psychology Today. Retrieved May 23, 2023, from https://www.psychologytoday.com/intl/blog/evil-deeds/200806/essential-secrets-psychotherapy-the-inner-child.

DiPietro JA, Costigan KA, Voegtline KM. Studies In Fetal Behavior: Revisited, Renewed, And Reimagined. *Monogr Soc Res Child Dev*. 2015 Sep;80(3):vii;1-94. doi: 10.1111/mono.v80.3. PMID: 26303396; PMCID: PMC4835043.

Imbir, K.K. (2017). Psychoevolutionary Theory of Emotion (Plutchik). In: Zeigler-Hill, V., Shackelford, T. (eds) Encyclopedia of Personality and Individual Differences. Springer, Cham. https://doi.org/10.1007/978-3-319-28099-8_547-1.

Murray, H. (2023). Transactional Analysis Theory & Therapy: Eric Berne. Simply Psychology. https://www.simplypsychology.org/transactional-analysis-eric-berne.html.

Pantic I. Online social networking and mental health. Cyberpsychol Behav Soc Netw. 2014 Oct;17(10):652-7. doi: 10.1089/cyber.2014.0070. Epub 2014 Sep 5. PMID: 25192305; PMCID: PMC4183915.

Persona – International Association of Analytical Psychology – IAAP. (n.d.). https://iaap.org/jung-analytical-psychology/short-articles-on-analytical-psychology/persona-2/#:~:text=As%20Jung%20says%2C%20%E2%80%9CThe%20persona,true%20nature%20of%20the%20individual.

Siegfried, W. (2014). The Formation and Structure of the Human Psyche: Id, Ego, and Super-Ego – The Dynamic (Libidinal) and Static Unconsciousness, Sublimation, and the Social Dimension of Identity Formation. *Athene Noctua: Undergraduate Philosophy Journal*, 2, 1–3. https://www.fau.edu/athenenoctua/pdfs/William%20Siegfried.pdf.

Van Driel, M. A. (2022, July 12). Projecting the Shadow Self is Surreptitiously Seeing Our Darkness in Others | CPTSDfoundation.org.

https://cptsdfoundation.org/2022/07/12/projecting-the-shadow-self-is-surreptitiously-seeing-our-darkness-in-others/.

Venniyoor, A. (2020). PTEN: A Thrifty Gene That Causes Disease in Times of Plenty? *Frontiers in Nutrition*, 7, 81. https://doi.org/10.3389/fnut.2020.00081

www.ingramcontent.com/pod-product-compliance
Lightning Source LLC
LaVergne TN
LVHW012019060526
838201LV00061B/4369